T·H·E
EXCELLENT
EMPIRE
+ + + + + + + + + + + + + + + +

OTHER BOOKS BY JAROSLAV PELIKAN:

Jesus Through the Centuries
The Christian Tradition (5 volumes)
The Vindication of Tradition
The Mystery of Continuity

Frontispiece portrait of Sir Edward Gibbon (engraved after original painting by Sir Joshua Reynolds) from the first volume of Gibbon's *The History of the Decline and Fall of the Roman Empire*, London, 1776. Photo by E. Bruce Howell, Courtesy of Doheny Library, University of Southern California, Los Angeles.

T·H·E
EXCELLENT
EMPIRE

+ + + + + + + + + + + + + + + + +

The Fall of Rome
And the Triumph of the Church

JAROSLAV PELIKAN

**THE RAUSCHENBUSCH LECTURES,
NEW SERIES, I**

1817

Harper & Row, Publishers, San Francisco

New York, Grand Rapids, Philadelphia, St. Louis
London, Singapore, Sydney, Tokyo, Toronto

The Rauschenbusch Lectures are sponsored by Colgate-Rochester Divinity School/ Bexley Hall/Crozer Theological Seminary, Rochester, NY.

FIRST HARPER & ROW PAPERBACK EDITION PUBLISHED IN 1990.

Library of Congress Cataloging-in-Publication Data

Pelikan, Jaroslav Jan
   The excellent empire.

   (The Rauschenbusch lectures ; new ser., 1)
   1. Rome—History—Empire, 284–476.   2. Fathers of the church.   3. Church history—Primitive and early church, ca. 30-600.   4. Gibbon, Edward, 1737–1794. History of the decline and fall of the Roman Empire.
I. Title.   II. Series.
DG312.P38   1987   937'.09   87-45194
ISBN 0-06-254636-8

ISBN 0-06-254867-0 (pbk.)
90   91   92   93   94   HAD   10   9   8   7   6   5   4   3   2   1

To Daniel J. Boorstin

The theologian may indulge the pleasing task of describing Religion as she descended from Heaven, arrayed in her native purity. A more melancholy duty is imposed on the historian. He must discover the inevitable mixture of error and corruption which she contracted in a long residence upon earth, among a weak and degenerate race of beings.

Contents

Preface

This book is the outcome of the Walter Rauschenbusch Lectures I delivered at the Colgate-Rochester Divinity School in the closing days of March 1984. Inaugurated in 1931 to honor the most important exponent of the theology of the social gospel, Walter Rauschenbusch (1861–1918), who was a professor at Colgate-Rochester, the lectureship deals with the application of the ethic of the Christian gospel to the needs and problems of society.

In introducing my own Rauschenbusch Lectures, therefore, I expressed the fear that I might be delivering them under false pretenses, for I admitted that I am by no means as sure as a Rauschenbusch Lecturer probably ought to be that the social gospel was the most important reinterpretation of the Christian faith in the twentieth century. When Rauschenbusch, in a chapter entitled "Why Has Christianity Never Undertaken the Work of Social Reconstruction?" in his *Christianity and the Social Crisis,* listed sacramentalism, asceticism, and especially dogma as the forces that "deflect" Christianity from its proper mission, he was attacking the very forces I have been studying for my entire scholarly life.

But I am consoled by the sense that there may be some reciprocity in all of this, for in April 1917 Rauschenbusch delivered the lectures that were to become *A Theology for the Social Gospel* as the Nathaniel William Taylor Lectures at Yale. In his foreword he acknowledged that "the Taylor Lectures are expected to deal with some theme in Doctrinal Theology," but explained that "the [Yale] Faculty in their invitation indicated that a discussion of some phase of the social problem would be welcome." Similarly, the faculty of the Colgate-Rochester Divinity School indicated that since Rauschenbusch was a historian by training, some themes from the history of theology, and even from the history of dogma, would be welcome.

As many readers will recognize, the title of the second chapter is borrowed from the third set of the Rauschenbusch Lectures, delivered and published in 1933 by Shirley Jackson Case, dean of the Divinity School of the University of Chicago. There is very little overlapping in the method or content of Dean Case's *The Social Triumph of the Ancient Church* and mine—and, I am afraid, still less overlapping in the point of view. I have approached the question of what Case called "the social triumph of the ancient church" from the perspective of what Edward Gibbon called "the triumph of barbarism and religion," asking whether these "triumphs" (if that is indeed the right word for them) were identical. Christian responses to the "fall of Rome" provided the basis (or the foil) for Gibbon's account, not only in the celebrated fifteenth and sixteenth chapters of the *Decline and Fall* but throughout the seventy-one chapters of the book.

My reading of Gibbon began more than fifty years ago. Over the years, my teachers—and then my own students, the audiences at my public lectures, and the readers of my books—have repeatedly commented on the traces, both good and bad, that this chronic exposure to his narrative has left on my style as well as on my thought. And as I have recently said elsewhere, it was probably Gibbon's *Decline and Fall* in unlikely combination with Ralph Waldo Emerson's *Representative Men* through which as a boy my ambition was pointed in the direction of becoming a historian.

Yet except for two seminars (one for Yale undergraduates in Pierson College, the other for the executive officers and editors of Harper & Row, Publishers), my first public opportunity to present the outcome of my "lucubrations" (to use one of Gibbon's favorite words) on the subject of Gibbon's *History of the Decline and Fall of the Roman Empire* came only in 1975. In preparation for the bicentennial to be shared in 1976 by the American Republic and the first volume of the *Decline and Fall* (as well as Adam Smith's *Wealth of Nations*), the director of the Woodrow Wilson International Center for Scholars in Washington, James H. Billington, invited me to join with several other friends and colleagues (including William H. McNeill) in an examination of Gibbon. Subsequently I published brief notices on the theme in *Harper's* and in *Daedalus*.

Since that bicentennial (and in anticipation of the bicentennial in 1988 of the completion of the *Decline and Fall*), I have had the opportunity to expand my reflections on one or another part of this material under the auspices of several lectureships in addition to the Rauschenbusch: the Solomon Katz Lecture at the University of Washington, the Biever Memorial Lectures at Loyola University in New Orleans, the Cross Current Lecture Series at the University of Michigan, the Pope John Paul II Lecture at Trinity College in Washington, D.C., the Leon Lecture at the University of Pennsylvania, the President's Lectures at the New York Public Library, the Mead-Swing Lectures at Oberlin College—and, revising all of these one last time, the William Clyde Devane Lectures at Yale.

In keeping both with the lecture format and with the precedent of most earlier Rauschenbusch Lectures, I have resisted my strong inclination to turn this into a fully documented monograph, and instead of an ongoing debate with other scholars I have mentioned in the footnotes only a few of the works on which I have most depended or from which I have most dissented. For the same reasons, classical, biblical, and patristic sources are cited in the standard manner, enabling readers to locate the passage in any edition or translation; some of the renderings are my own, while others are from existing translations. Citations from Gibbon's *Decline and Fall* include the chapter number (to facilitate consulting other editions) and the volume and page in J. B. Bury's edition (7 vols.; London, 1896–1900) and retain the original spelling and punctuation. The epigraphs to the several sections of the book all come from Gibbon.

The dedication of this book is the expression of a friendship and collegiality that goes back, as so much of my intellectual life does, to the University of Chicago, where a quarter of a century or more ago Daniel J. Boorstin and I taught and wrote history and went on learning history—and discussed the great historians, including Edward Gibbon, with his quaint comments about the difference between the theologian and the historian.

INTRODUCTION

. . . to deduce the most important circumstances of its decline and fall: a revolution which will ever be remembered, and is still felt by the nations of the earth.

CHAPTER 1

The Fall of Rome
as Historical Paradigm

1776 was a vintage year for social thought—if not a very good year for empires. At least three major documents of political, social, and economic reflection were published in the English-speaking world during that year: most memorable of all, "A Declaration by the Representatives of the United States of America in Congress Assembled, July 4, 1776," the Declaration of Independence, written by Thomas Jefferson; *An Inquiry into the Nature and Causes of the Wealth of Nations,* by Adam Smith; and the first volume of *The History of the Decline and Fall of the Roman Empire,* by Edward Gibbon. Each of these writings has had a major part to play in the history of modern thought. Not only do all three of them appear in the fifty-one-volume set *Great Books of the Western World,* within which Adam Smith occupies one entire volume and Edward Gibbon two entire volumes (Aristotle, Thomas Aquinas, and Shakespeare are the only other authors to have been allocated two volumes each);[1] but all three would, almost without any question, qualify for inclusion as part of any such secular "canon." In addition to being contemporaneous and to having been written in the English language, the Declaration of Independence and *The Wealth of Nations* also have in common with *The Decline and Fall of the Roman Empire* an awareness of what the latter book's author called "the memorable series of revolutions which, in the course of about thirteen centuries, gradually undermined, and at length destroyed, the fabric of human greatness."[2] It was an awareness shared by other contemporary and near-contemporary thinkers.

Thus Edmund Burke, whom the Declaration of Independence

had moved to speak in 1777 about "the difficulty of reconciling the strong presiding power, that is so useful towards the conservation of a vast, disconnected, infinitely diversified empire, with that liberty and safety of the provinces, which they must enjoy (in opinion and practice at least) or they will not be provinces at all,"[3] was prompted by the events of the French Revolution a few years later to reflect more deeply on that difficulty. And when he did so, it was "the memorable series of revolutions" associated with the decline and fall of Rome that came to his mind. "Paris," he suggested near the end of his *Reflections on the Revolution in France*, "stands in the place of antient [*sic*] Rome," specifically in dealing with the "difficulty" about which he had spoken in response to the American Revolution, for Paris, like ancient Rome, found itself in the parasitical position of being "maintained by the subject provinces." This was, Burke believed, "an evil inevitably attendant on the dominion of sovereign democratic republics," evil because of the inherent contradiction between, on the one hand, their exercising a "dominion" that was "sovereign" over their provinces and, on the other hand, their claiming still to be "democratic republics." It was a lesson of Roman history—and, he was obviously implying, of French history and of British history as well—that this evil could "survive that republican domination which gave rise to it." When that happened, "despotism itself must submit to the vices of popularity,"[4] or, as we would say now, using an English word that was invented only in the late nineteenth century and in America rather than in England, the vices of populism.[5] "And this unnatural combination," Burke solemnly declared, "was one great cause of her [Rome's] ruin."[6] His countryman and contemporary Edward Gibbon had, just two years earlier, published the final volume of a work in whose opening chapter, after a guided tour of the provinces, he had spoken of a similar phenomenon in the Roman Empire:

This long enumeration of provinces, whose broken fragments have formed so many powerful kingdoms, might almost induce us to forgive the vanity or ignorance of the ancients. Dazzled with the extensive sway, the irresistible strength, and the real or affected moderation of the emperors, they permitted themselves to despise, and sometimes to forget the outlying countries which had been left in the enjoyment of a barbarous independence; and they gradually assumed the licence of confounding the Roman monarchy with the globe of the earth.[7]

Gibbon's work can be read, at least in part, as a documentation of Burke's thesis.

The countryman and contemporary who published *The Wealth of Nations* in 1776 was pursuing other "difficulties" than those occupying the moral and political philosophy of Edmund Burke. In Book Three, after having considered labor and its productivity in Book One and stock and capital in Book Two, Adam Smith turned to a comparative examination of what he called "the different progress of opulence in different nations," by which he meant particularly the relation between agricultural and urban economies. His case study for this comparative examination was the decline and fall of the Roman Empire:

When the German and Scythian nations overran the western provinces of the Roman empire, the confusions which followed so great a revolution lasted for several centuries. The rapine and violence which the barbarians exercised against the ancient inhabitants interrupted the commerce between the towns and the country. The towns were deserted, and the country was left uncultivated, and the western provinces of Europe, which had enjoyed a considerable degree of opulence under the Roman empire, sunk into the lowest state of poverty and barbarism.[8]

He then proceeded to review the economic effects of "the confusions which followed so great a revolution." Having pointed out earlier how the imperial system of taxation had brought it about that Rome was importing most of its grain instead of growing it in Italy,[9] he observed here that this had "obstructed the cultivation of ancient Italy, naturally the most fertile country in Europe, and at that time the seat of the greatest empire in the world." This "ancient policy" was "unfavourable to the improvement and cultivation of land," and, with the revolution brought on by the fall of "the greatest empire in the world," the inevitable result was "the discouragement of agriculture in the ancient state of Europe after the fall of the Roman empire." Although, as he went on to note, "the inhabitants of cities and towns were, after the fall of the Roman empire, not more favoured than those of the country," it turned out nevertheless that "order and good government, and along with them the liberty and security of individuals, were . . . established in cities at a time when the occupiers of land in the country were exposed to every sort of violence." And he found it noteworthy that "the first manufactures for distant sale . . . seem to have been established in the western provinces of Europe after the fall of the Roman empire."[10]

It is not necessary to agree either with Edmund Burke's or with Adam Smith's diagnosis to recognize that for both of them the fall of Rome had assumed the status of a historical paradigm by which other historical developments, including the historical developments of their own time, could be illuminated. The history of Rome was playing that role even in the thought of a contemporary of Burke, Smith, and Gibbon who believed that "the experience of other nations will afford little instruction" for contemporary politics and who therefore disparaged what he called "the dim light of historical research." Those were the words of Alexander Hamilton in Number 70 of *The Federalist,* dated 15 March 1788, the very year in which the final volumes of the *Decline and Fall* were published. Between those two statements he managed to summarize in one trenchant paragraph the lessons to be derived from a study of the paradigm of Rome for a consideration of what he called "plurality in the executive." There were, Hamilton noted, many cases in "the Roman history" to document "the mischiefs to the republic from the dissensions between the consuls, and between the military tribunes, who were at times substituted to the consuls." By contrast, however, the history of Rome "gives us no specimens of any peculiar advantages derived to the state, from the circumstances of the plurality of those magistrates," since there were in fact no such "advantages."[11]

In a parallel to Gibbon's statement (to which we shall be returning) that "instead of inquiring why the Roman empire was destroyed, we should rather be surprised that it had subsisted so long,"[12] Hamilton declared it to be "a matter of astonishment" not that this system of plurality in the executive sometimes led to conflict and bloodshed, but "that the dissentions between them were not more frequent, or more fatal." What prevented this unwieldy system from creating anarchy was "the prudent policy" adopted by various pairs of consuls "of making a division of government between them." And then, "after the arms of the republic had considerably expanded the bounds of its empire," they even adopted as "an established custom" a division not only of administrative responsibility, but of territorial authority, with one consul "remaining at Rome to govern the city and its environs" while his colleague assumed "the command in the more distant provinces." "This expedient," Hamilton concluded with perhaps a touch of wryness, "must no doubt have had great influence in preventing those collisions and rivalships, which might otherwise have embroiled the peace of the republic." All in all, that must be acknowledged as a remarkably astute piece of "historical research" into the Roman republic for someone who believed that such research could at best cast only a "dim light" on the question of plurality in the executive as this question confronted the infant American republic; and the founding fathers of the United States did indeed benefit from the "instruction" that had come from "the experience of other nations."[13]

Among the founding fathers, James Madison would appear to have been less diffident than Alexander Hamilton about deriving such instruction from ancient history. Madison devoted an entire early number of the *Federalist*, which was dated 7 December 1787 and written with Hamilton's assistance, to an examination, on the basis of Plutarch and other classical historians, of what he himself termed the "very instructive analogy" between the confederacy of Greek republics and "the present confederation of the American States"; and in speaking of the Achean League he expressed his regret "that such imperfect monuments remain of this curious political fabric," because, he surmised, "it is probable that more light would be thrown by it on the science of federal government, than by any of the like experiments with which we are acquainted."[14] If the political history of Greece in its flowering was so "instructive" for the invention of the new federal structure of the United States, it bore less analogy to the military situation of the new American republic; as Hamilton had noted a few weeks earlier, "standing armies [did not] spring up out of the contentions which so often distracted the ancient republics of Greece," because "the true condition of the people of those republics" had been to be "a nation of soldiers," a condition that was incompatible with "the industrious habits of the people of the present day," at any rate in America.[15]

Rather it was to the military history of Rome, and specifically to the history of its decline and fall, that Madison turned for an "instructive analogy." For the Roman military had been the agent of the rise of the Roman Empire—and then it had become the instrument of its decline and fall. The lesson of the first part of that history was that an imbalance of military power threatened the political independence of the weaker states, so that in the fifteenth century, "the unhappy epoch of military establishments in time of peace," French rearmament had "forced" all Europe to arm as well. Otherwise "all Europe must long ago have worne the chains of a universal monarch," that is, of a French monarch. (Madison wrote this, it should be noted, less than a decade before the rise of Napoleon Bonaparte.) The classic case of such a military imbalance was, of course, ancient Rome. "The veteran legions of Rome," Madison observed, "were an overmatch for the undisciplined valour of all other nations"; and so it was that the legions of Rome "rendered her mistress of the world." That was, however, only the first half of the lesson. "Not less true is it," he continued, "that the liberties of Rome proved the final victim to her military triumphs." From the example of Rome it was clear that "a standing force . . . is a dangerous, at the same time that it may be a necessary provision."[16]

Gibbon had repeatedly drawn the same moral. Having explained in the very first chapter of the *Decline and Fall* how it was that "the safety and honour of the empire was principally intrusted to the legions,"[17] he went on in the third chapter to describe the threat that this posed:

The insolence of the armies inspired Augustus with fears of a still more alarming nature. The despair of the citizens could only attempt what the power of the soldiers was, at any time, able to execute. How precarious was his own authority over men whom he had taught to violate every social duty! He had heard their seditious clamours; he dreaded their calmer moments of reflection. . . . The troops professed the fondest attachment to the house of Caesar; but the attachments of the multitude are capricious and inconstant.[18]

Designating the civilian president of the United States as commander-in-chief of all the armed forces was a device calculated to obviate that very threat; and Lord Byron's well-known identification of George Washington as

> The Cincinnatus of the West,
> Whom envy dared not hate,[19]

recalled the archetypical civilian commander-in-chief Cincinnatus, the shadowy but apparently historical Roman who, according to tradition, had left the farm for sixteen days in 458 B.C.E., led the Romans to victory over their enemies, and then returned to his plow.

In this respect, as in so many others, Alexis de Tocqueville represented a considerably greater measure of sophistication about the possibilities but also the limitations in the uses of historical analogy. Nevertheless, he, too, had his mind on the decline and fall of the Roman Empire. In his chapter on "Why the Americans Are More Concerned with the Applications Than with the Theory of Science,"[20] Tocqueville pondered the special problems and the special opportunities that a democratic system of government posed for the study of science. He saw the principal problem as the excessively pragmatic approach characteristic of democratic, and specifically of American, scientific endeavor: "These same Americans who have never discovered a general law of mechanics have changed the face of the world by introducing a new machine for navigation," referring, of course, to the steamboat, of which he said elsewhere that it had "added unbelievably to the strength and prosperity of the Union."[21] But "confining ourselves to practice," Tocqueville warned, "we may lose sight of basic principles, and when these have been entirely forgotten, we may apply the methods derived from them badly." Therefore it was necessary to break with the slovenly intellectual habit of "perpetually concentrating attention on the minute examination of secondary effects" and to find ways "to distract it therefrom sometimes and lift it to the contemplation of first causes." To reinforce his warning that this lack of interest among Americans in "first causes" and in the theory and philosophy of science posed a threat from within to the integrity and the future of American civilization, he added: "Because Roman civilization perished through barbarian invasions, we are perhaps too much inclined to think that this is the only way a civilization can die." But, he noted ominously, "if the lights that guide us ever go out, they will fade little by little, as if of their own accord."

Yet it would be an oversimplification of Tocqueville's subtle analysis to forget that he turned to the classics of Greece and Rome particularly for their bearing on the cultivation precisely of those theoretical and literary interests whose absence he so lamented among educated Americans. He was convinced that "it may be good for the literature of one people to study that of another even though it has no bearing on their social and political needs." The education of most citizens in a democracy should, he argued, be "scientific, commercial, and industrial rather than literary"; presumably, this was especially true of American society. Yet on the other hand it was "important that those who are destined by nature or fate to adopt a literary career or to cultivate such tastes" should devote themselves above all to the classical literature of Greece and Rome. "All who have ambition to literary excellence in democratic nations," he summarized, "should ever refresh themselves at classical springs; that is the most wholesome medicine for the mind."[22]

Alexis de Tocqueville's *Democracy in America* was first published in Paris from 1835 to 1840. In 1843 Karl Marx came to Paris, having recently been converted to socialism, and almost a quarter of a century later, in 1867, he published the first volume of *Das Kapital.* Much of the historical research underlying *Das Kapital* had been done in the British Museum and concerned itself with British industry and British labor. But Marx drew his examples from an astonishing variety of historical sources, ancient, medieval, and modern. Thus in Part Eight, Chapter 27 of *Das Kapital,* describing what happens in the "expropriation of agricultural population" when the relatively free yeomen, who have been supporting themselves from the land, have it taken away from them and are reduced to the status of a proletariat, he quoted a passage from Appian's *Civil Wars* with the comment: "We are reminded of ancient Rome." Then he added, in a manner reminiscent of the comments quoted earlier from Gibbon and from the American founding fathers in *The Federalist:* "Military service . . . hastened to so great an extent the ruin of the Roman plebeians."[23]

In the aftermath of World War I, Oswald Spengler published *The Decline of the West [Der Untergang des Abendlandes]* between 1918 and 1922, in which much of the pessimism of the postwar period found one of its most eloquent expressions. Spengler applied to the history of Western civilization the metaphor of organic growth—and of organic decay—and concluded that the vitalities from which this civilization had been nourished for centuries were now exhausted. Spengler's larger thesis as well as the many responses to him cannot be our concern here. What is of interest is that Spengler's diagnosis (or, as it would be more proper to term it, his autopsy) of Western civilization was an obvious extrapolation from the traditional preoccupation with the "fall of Rome." As he says on the very first page, "the decline of the West, which at first sight may appear, like the corresponding decline of the Classical Culture, a phenomenon limited in time and space, we now perceive to be a philosophical problem that, when comprehended in all its gravity, includes within itself every great question of Being." And a little later he advances

the hypothesis that "considered in itself, the Roman world-domin-
ion was a negative phenomenon. . . . That the Romans did *not*
conquer the world is certain; they merely took possession of a booty
that lay open to everyone." And it was a general rule "that *Imperial-
ism* . . . is to be taken as the typical symbol of the passing away."
Therefore, he concludes,

the Imperium Romanum appears no longer as an isolated phenomenon, but
as the normal product of a strict and energetic, megalopolitan, predomi-
nantly practical spirituality, as typical of a final and irreversible condition
which has occurred often enough though it has only been identified as
such in this instance.[24]

Because it "has only been identified as such in this instance," it was
necessary to generalize from the phenomenon of the Roman Empire
to the "final and irreversible condition" of other phenomena, including the modern West.

But where the usual efforts to explain how Rome had fallen,
including the several with which we are dealing in this book, had
usually been based within a later culture, whether medieval or
modern, by which Rome in its decline and fall had been implicitly
measured, Spengler's *Decline of the West* claimed, at least in principle,
not to make the present a norm for the understanding of the past,
but to be examining the present itself as a symptom of the decline.
In the present he found the unmistakable signs of a "luxury" that
was the manifestation of an incurable decadence. Interestingly,
many of the specific social and moral phenomena to which Spengler
pointed as evidence—self-indulgence, loss of civic responsibility,
failure of nerve—were the very same ones that the interpreters of
the decline and fall of Rome had long employed in their attempts
to trace back from the events of the fourth and fifth centuries to the
root causes of the political, social, and moral eclipse of classical
culture. Spengler himself acknowledged that he was working from
Rome as the model for the decline of a civilization.

Similarly, the author of one of the most instructive books of the
twentieth century on revolution, Hannah Arendt, found herself, in
Marx's phrase, "reminded of ancient Rome." Discussing what she
called "the incredible ease with which governments would be overthrown" in the modern period, she went on to describe "the break-
down of the old Roman trinity of religion, tradition, and authority."
In its "innermost principle," this trinity had, she maintained, "sur-

vived the change of the Roman Republic into the Roman Empire, as it was to survive the change of the Roman Empire into the Holy Roman Empire." Only with "the onslaught of the modern age" did this principle itself fall to pieces.[25] Although she was chiefly interested in the discontinuity between this "modern age" and all preceding ages of Western civilization, Hannah Arendt had to be "reminded of ancient Rome" simply because one of the most fascinating aspects of the revolution accompanying the decline and fall of the Roman Empire was the preservation of a vast amount of continuity. As Gibbon said in one of his summaries (which will engage us at the conclusion of this book), the "inestimable gifts" of Roman civilization, identified by him elsewhere as "language, religion, and laws,"[26] had been spared in the fall of Rome and therefore "have been successfully propagated," so that "they can never be lost"[27]—at least not until the age of which Hannah Arendt was writing.

Gibbon's "memorable series of revolutions" may therefore be seen as an abiding paradigm and a continuing preoccupation. He was not the first to reflect about the meaning of this paradigm, nor yet the last. This book is an effort to read Gibbon's history in the light of *its* history, on the basis of the most memorable of the responses to the decline and fall of the Roman Empire by its Christian contemporaries. To that end, the book plays off two designations of those events against each other. The first, summarizing the contemporary patristic reactions, is taken from the title of the third set of the distinguished series of Rauschenbusch Lectures at Colgate-Rochester Divinity School, delivered in 1933 by the church historian Shirley Jackson Case of the University of Chicago and published in that same year as *The Social Triumph of the Ancient Church.* These lectures, it has been said by Case's colleagues, "represent the . . . pioneering of his mind with social-historical methodology in the broad areas of early church history and the development of Christian thought."[28] The second designation, summarizing Edward Gibbon's reaction to those patristic reactions, comes from the final chapter of the *Decline and Fall:* "The Triumph of Barbarism and Religion."[29] The historical counterpoint between these two drastically different views of "triumph," together with the unavoidable consideration of the ambiguity in the very question of "triumph or tragedy," may perhaps stand as a fitting recognition of the permanent value in the paradigm of "the fall of Rome."

Part One

THE DECLINE AND FALL
OF THE ROMAN EMPIRE

His [Augustine's] learning is too often borrowed, and his arguments are too often not his own; but the whole work claims the merit of a magnificent design, vigorously, and not unskillfully, executed.

CHAPTER 2

The Social Triumph of the Ancient Church

To the victor, it has often been said, belong the spoils. It is likewise to the victor that there usually belongs the privilege of providing both the definitive historical narrative of *how* the triumph was achieved and the official explanation of *why* it came out as it did: we have very little information from the inhabitants of any of the *partes tres* of Gaul about what happened in the Gallic War, but we do have in Julius Caesar's *Gallic War* an account that still informs historians. And almost no one but a scholar can recite any of the speeches of Jefferson Davis, while the Gettysburg Address of Abraham Lincoln stands not only as a monument of American rhetoric but as a commentary on the battle of Gettysburg and on the entire War Between the States that is by now inseparable from our common memory of the events themselves.

To speak about the decline and fall of the Roman Empire as "the social triumph of the ancient church" is to look at the events associated with that "memorable revolution" (in Gibbon's own memorable phrase) through the eyes of the victors. The thoroughness of the victors has often seen to it that there remains no other way for us to view those events. Not only are we, for this period as for so many others throughout most of human history, denied access to the minds of ordinary people as they watched this history in the making and forced to depend on the documents provided by various of the élites of the fourth and fifth centuries, but among the documents of those élites, only some have been permitted to survive. For example, most students of the early Christian centuries would probably concur in the judgment that among the documents of the pagan intellectual élite in the Greco-Roman world one of the most able philosophical and theological critiques of Christianity was the treatise *The True Doctrine,* written by a man named Celsus and answered for the Christians sometime during the late 240s by Origen of Alexandria in his treatise *Contra Celsum.* Yet, as Henry Chadwick says, "We must . . . conclude that we know nothing of Origen's opponent except what can be inferred from the text of Origen himself"[1]—and that means we know nothing whatsoever about him, neither the dates of his life, nor the philosophical school (or schools) to which he may have adhered, nor the places where he lived and died. And we can reconstruct his attack on the church only from Origen's reply, thanks to the widespread literary convention (undoubtedly related in part to the limited circulation of such works before the advent of printing) of quoting *in extenso* from one's opponent before replying. Even the documents produced by the governmental élite of pagan Rome became the victims of the victors. The emperor Julian (to whom the Christians gave the surname "the Apostate") forms the subject, as "a young and valiant hero," of one of Gibbon's most skillful biographical essays.[2] Many of Julian's official and personal papers have survived. Yet for his continuation of the pagan critique of Christianity in the tradition of Celsus we are, once again, completely dependent on the Christian counterattack, written in this case by another Christian Alexandrian, the patriarch Cyril, who died in 444.

To the victor belong the spoils—and the history. And when a later historian, even one of the most celebrated of later historians, undertakes to recast the narrative of "the social triumph of the ancient church" by viewing it from the perspective of the vanquished rather than of the victor and consequently by describing it as "the triumph of barbarism and religion" instead, such a historical reconstruction is still largely dependent on what has survived, or more precisely, on what the victors have permitted to survive and what their successors have gone on to edit and collect. Gibbon depended for some of his narrative on the French Benedictine scholar of the Congregation of Saint Maur (hence their appellation "Maurists"), Jean Mabillon, who had died in 1707, thirty years before Gibbon was born. "The learned Mabillon," as Gibbon refers to him, was one of the "great masters of ecclesiastical science" and, at least on occasion, "seems to be inspired by the genius of humanity."[3] Even more than the editions of Mabillon and other Maurists, it was the sixteen volumes of source materials collected in the *Mé-*

moires pour servir à l'histoire ecclésiastique des six premiers siècles by an earlier French priest and ecclesiastical historian, Louis Sébastien le
Nain de Tillemont, on which Gibbon, despite his prejudices, was
obliged to depend as the work of a "learned compiler,"[4] who had
"compile[d] the lives of the saints with incredible patience and
religious accuracy."[5] He was "indefatigable but partial," "offended
with the air of Paganism [in Constantine] which seems unworthy
of a Christian Prince," and excessively "fond of increasing [his]
stock of miracles."[6] Tillemont's learned compilations went as far
as the age of Justinian, at which point Gibbon was on his own.
"Once more, and almost for the last time," he wrote, "I appeal to
the diligence of Tillemont."[7] "And here," he wrote a few pages
later in grudging but sincere tribute from one historian to another,
"I must take leave for ever of that incomparable guide—whose
bigotry is balanced by the merits of erudition, diligence, veracity,
and scrupulous minuteness."[8] Perhaps the weakest part of the *Decline and Fall of the Roman Empire* is Gibbon's treatment of the history
of the Byzantine Empire, which he viewed as "a tedious and uniform tale of weakness and misery."[9] That notorious shortcoming
in Gibbon's narrative is certainly due at least in part to Tillemont's
having been prevented by death from finishing his compilation,
although Gibbon's own political and theological prejudices also
made their contribution.

One of the longest sections of Tillemont's *Mémoires Ecclésiastiques,*
the entire thirteenth volume comprising more than a thousand
pages, is devoted to Augustine; "the diligence of that learned Jan-
senist," Gibbon comments, "was excited on this occasion by fac-
tious and devout zeal for the founder of his sect,"[10] since the *Augus-
tinus* of Cornelius Jansen had been devoted to claiming the authority
of Augustine for its doctrines of sin and grace. On the basis of
Tillemont's account, Gibbon summarized the life and works of
Augustine in only one paragraph (despite some references elsewhere), adding the rather surprising admission: "My personal acquaintance with the bishop of Hippo does not extend beyond the
Confessions and the *City of God.*"[11] Earlier, in speaking about "the
grave and learned Augustin," he had, again on the basis of Tillemont, characterized the *City of God:*

His learning is too often borrowed, and his arguments are too often not
his own; but the whole work claims the merit of a magnificent design,
vigorously, and not unskillfully, executed.[12]

At least the second part of that characterization, the phrase "magnificent design, vigorously, and not unskillfully, executed," would be an apt description of Gibbon's *Decline and Fall,* which plays out its account of "the triumph of barbarism and religion" in counterpoint with the accounts of "the social triumph of the ancient church" set down by Augustine and other church fathers. To avoid the danger (to which modern social history is no less liable than is modern intellectual history) of superimposing later categories, in this case the categories of twentieth-century social science, on an earlier period and thus, for example, of reducing the history of the ancient church to an account of a class struggle, it may be helpful to adopt the categories that the ancient church adopted in describing itself and to interpret its "social triumph" in that framework.

By far the most widely used such self-description from the ancient church and one that continues to be recited in the liturgy by millions of Christians all over the world achieved its definitive formulation at the end of the fourth or the beginning of the fifth century, thus in the very period with which we are dealing here. It appears in what is generally known as "the Nicene Creed," a questionable designation, however, since in its present form it was not in fact adopted at the Council of Nicea in 325; the creed is known more frequently in scholarly literature as "the Niceno-Constantinopolitan Creed," although that designation too is questionable. It is in any case the only statement of faith genuinely entitled to the term "ecumenical creed." In the "Nicene Creed" the church is confessed to be "one, holy, catholic, and apostolic [*unam, sanctam, catholicam et apostolicam*]." That fourfold specification of the "notes of the church" went on to have a history of its own in all the subsequent centuries of Christian history, and for the history of the theological doctrine of the church, also in its periods of crisis, it remains the most useful of all formulas.[13] But the four "notes"— unity, holiness, catholicity, and apostolicity—were no less a description of the social thought of the church, even when their application to the "spotted actuality" of the empirical church became highly problematical, as it often did.

Although the designation *holy* was the first of the four to appear in a creedal document, it was with the identification of the church as *one* that this standard formula began. It is likewise with the church as one that the earliest systematic consideration we have of the nature of the church, the *De unitate* [On Unity] of Cyprian of

Carthage from the middle of the third century, is primarily concerned. The admonitions of Cyprian's essay make it clear that "unity" here was by no means only a part of the creed or an abstract theological concept removed from the realities of social and economic life, but a practical function in the concrete life of the Christian community. Contrasting the way the unity of the church had been expressed in the New Testament era, when "they used to give for sale houses and estates . . . and presented to the apostles the price of them, to be distributed for the use of the poor," with the present loss of concern about the poor, Cyprian warned that "unanimity is diminished in proportion as liberality of working is decayed."[14] While it may be an arbitrary imposition of later social categories to force the history of these centuries into the pattern of the class struggle, it clearly is a valid application of the concept of "class" to see in such exhortations as Cyprian's the social struggle of the early church with the issues of poverty and property in the late Roman Empire.

In a chapter entitled "Christianity and Worldly Goods," the author of *The Social Triumph of the Ancient Church,* Shirley Jackson Case, describes the history of the process by which "in the course of three centuries the original indifference of Christians toward worldly goods had been completely supplanted by a determination on the part of the church to bring the material resources of the world into the service of religion." But that change did not in any way entail the surrender of the "unity of the church" on which Cyprian had put such great emphasis specifically in connection with the Christian use of "the material resources of the world." On the contrary, as Case continues, "the effort was transfused by the Christian ideal of brotherhood and glorified by the devotion of the Christian communities to charitable activities."[15] That "Christian ideal of brotherhood" had been voiced in one of the Pauline epistles through the use of a series of contrasts in which the chronological sequence of Christian social developments in subsequent history was adumbrated:[16] "There is neither Jew nor Greek, there is neither slave nor free, there is neither male nor female; for you are all one in Christ Jesus" (Gal. 3:28). Each of those developments, moreover, represented an area of Roman society in which "the social triumph of the ancient church" as expressed through the unity of the church was to make itself manifest.

For the ancient church of the first century, the central social

question for the definition of unity was the first of these three, the
relation between Jews and non-Jews. It cannot be emphasized too
strongly or too often that Jesus and all of his apostles were Jews, but
that most or all of the leadership of the Christian community of the
second century—and probably also most or all of its membership—
came increasingly from Gentile ranks. The epistles of Paul and the
Acts of the Apostles are the documentation of the struggle among
what Wayne Meeks has called "the first urban Christians"[17] to
achieve a unity between Jew and Greek within the new reality
called the church of Christ. Initially that unity was defined and
dictated by the Jewish members of the community: Jewish dietary
laws applied to Christians no less than to (other) Jews, and a young
convert to Christianity, Timothy, was, we are told, "circumcised
. . . because of the Jews that were in those places, for they all knew
that his father was a Greek" (Acts 16:3). The question of whether
to apply all of the ceremonial laws of the Hebrew Bible and perhaps
the laws that had developed within the Jewish tradition after the
Hebrew Bible as well agitated the ancient church and provided the
occasion for the first "church council" as reported in the fifteenth
chapter of the Book of Acts. Its "decree" resolving the question,
which opened with the portentous words, "It has seemed good to
the Holy Spirit and to us," expressed the wish "to lay upon you no
greater burden than these necessary things." The four specific "necessary things" were: "that you abstain from what has been sac-
rificed to idols and from blood and from what is strangled and from
unchastity" (Acts 15:28–29). The textual variants in the transmission of the Greek text of this decree provide evidence of the confusion about its provisions that must have prevailed in large sections
of the church, especially during the centuries that followed; but
even more dramatic evidence for that confusion comes from the
juxtaposition in the decree of three kinds of dietary prohibition
(meat offered to idols, meat still in its blood, and meat that has not
been butchered in accordance with kosher prescriptions) with the
prohibition of sexual immorality—all four of these, one might conclude from the words themselves though mistakenly, on the same
level of being "necessary" requirements of Christian behavior.

In the event, of course, all of these dietary laws as well as the
law of circumcision became a dead letter as the Christian community became less and less Jewish both in its constituency and in its
patterns of life and worship. For our purposes here, the most impor-

tant implication of that radical transformation was this: the "ancient church" that was to achieve a "social triumph" over the Roman Empire was a Gentile church whose members were not ethnically or racially different from their Roman fellow citizens. Propaganda by Christian reformers in later centuries often romanticized the ancient church as an embodiment of every ideal, but the documents of the New Testament make it clear that whatever "unity" there may have been did not come easily. The two epistles of Paul to the church at Corinth are a particularly vivid description of the many kinds of disunity and discord that could arise: party spirit, tension between richer and poorer members, sexual scandal, drunkenness in the very celebration of the Lord's Supper, and more. It is necessary only to read the eloquent sermons delivered by John Chrysostom at the end of the fourth century in Antioch and in Constantinople to get a graphic picture of how such evils continued to prevail and even to flourish in the metropolitan Christianity that had achieved its "social triumph" over the empire.[18] The unity of the church, therefore, was not in any simple sense an empirical unity—certainly not a uniformity. Rather, the "unity" in the name of which—and by the force of which—Christianity prevailed over the empire was a unity defined not by membership in a *gens* (a nation or tribe) or by social class (social heterogeneity marked the Christian communities throughout the Mediterranean world) or by gender (unlike Mithraism, Christianity was not restricted to males), but by common adherence to the person of Jesus Christ and to the church that he was believed to have established.

When the ancient creeds spoke of the church as *holy,* that too was a characteristic that could not be defined in simple empirical terms. As J. N. D. Kelly says:

The connotation of the word "holy," like that of the parallel word "saints" so frequent in New Testament Christian parlance, has nothing to do, in the first instance at any rate, with *de facto* goodness of character or moral integrity. The Church is described as HOLY in the creed because it has been chosen by God, because He has predestined it to a glorious inheritance, and because He dwells in it in the Person of the Holy Spirit.[19]

That judgment about the theological doctrine of the church applies no less to its social teaching. But the development of such a theological doctrine was in fact the consequence of an evolution in the social teachings of the church. Initially, Christian writers had often drawn the contrast between the church and Roman society along moral lines. They took advantage of the moral satires of Roman writers such as Juvenal and Martial to describe the debauchery and sexual license of paganism as a reenactment of conditions before the Deluge.[20] Within the church itself, meanwhile, there were repeated efforts to impose, or if need be to reimpose, strict moral standards and to enforce them. The moral rigorism of Tertullian at the end of the second century directed itself against such moral abuses as the remarriage of widows or widowers, demanding that the difference between Christian behavior and the norms of ordinary Roman society be drawn as sharply as possible.

Such moral rigorism provides the historian of Christian social thought with data about conditions within the Christian movement of the second and third centuries. Perhaps the most significant body of such data came out of the behavior of believers under the conditions of persecution, particularly during the persecution instituted by the emperor Decius in the year 250 C.E. Although this campaign against the church by the Roman emperor produced its share of authentic martyrs, including Origen of Alexandria, who died a few years later as a consequence of tortures he had endured in the Decian persecution, it produced a major social crisis within the church as well. Under the threat of physical suffering or death, many Christians, including some of the clergy, collaborated with the enemy, coming to be known as "the lapsed": some of them actually participated in sacrifices to the gods or to the emperor and in other acts of pagan worship, while others were guilty of surrendering sacred books and other holy objects to the Roman soldiers. When the fire had passed and the smoke had cleared, the disciplinary structure of the Christian community was confronted with a major social-administrative and intellectual-theological dilemma. If the holiness of the church and of its members was to be defined as an empirically identifiable moral reality, it could not continue to tolerate within its midst those who had so fundamentally betrayed it in crisis. Yet the demand for holiness had, from the beginning, existed in tension with the offer of forgiveness. In fact, the pagan critic Celsus had satirized the Christian emphasis on forgiveness with this biting contrast:

Those who summon people to the other mysteries make this preliminary proclamation: "Whosoever has pure hands and a wise tongue." And again, others say: "Whosoever is pure from all defilement, and whose soul knows nothing of evil, and who has lived well and righteously." Such are the preliminary exhortations of those who promise purification from sins. But let us hear what folk these Christians call. "Whosoever is a sinner," they say, "whosoever is unwise, whosoever is a child, and, in a word, whosoever is a wretch, the kingdom of God will receive him."[21]

But now it was those who were already members of the community itself, not the outsiders, to whom it was necessary to apply simultaneously the standard of holiness and the offer of forgiveness.

The initial resolution of this dilemma during the second half of the third century, thus in the generations immediately preceding the "social triumph" associated with the conversion of the emperor Constantine, was to devise a series of penitential satisfactions by which lapsed members guilty of compromise under persecution could win restoration to the society of the church, but to hold clergy and bishops to a higher moral standard, thus making their holiness a guarantee of the holiness of the church. Eventually, however, the guarantee came to depend not on either the members or the clergy but on the objective holiness that reposed in the sacraments and was conferred by them. It was the achievement of Augustine as both theologian and administrator to provide the official formulation of this definition of holiness and to ensure its success. Viewed as a theological achievement, it created many problems, as becomes evident from the recurrence throughout the Middle Ages and the Reformation of the demand that the members of the clergy, and especially the clergy, manifest a genuine holiness of life, instead of relying on the "automatic [ex opere operato]" power of the sacraments. But as a social theory, it provided a definition of the holiness of the church that prepared it well for the responsibilities it was to assume after its "social triumph" over the Roman Empire. The church was not a moral all-star team for which one could qualify by being an athlete of holiness; it was a moral hospital in which, by the medicine of the sacraments, one could be gradually healed—provided that one subjected oneself to the discipline of the doctors and nurses.

The church had prepared itself for the responsibilities of its "social triumph" also by becoming *catholic.* Perhaps it will not be inappropriate to repeat here an earlier definition of catholicity as "identity plus universality. By 'identity' I mean that which distinguishes the church from the world—its message, its uniqueness, its particularity. By 'universality,' on the other hand, I mean that which impels the church to embrace nothing less than all mankind in its vision and in its appeal."[22] Because of that universal vision, there is certainly a sense in which only a world church could claim to be truly "catholic" and therefore a sense in which the Christian diffusion throughout most of the Roman Empire by the time of its decline and fall was the process by which the church had become "catholic." One can go even further and say that the ancient church achieved its "social triumph" by becoming "catholic," but that, conversely, it was enabled to become "catholic" by the very process of having achieved that "social triumph." At the same time, the definition of "catholicity" as "identity plus universality" implies that such a universal vision could not come at the expense of the particularity that distinguished the church from other societies. During the first three or four centuries, therefore, the social thought of the ancient church may be said to have been engaged in a twofold strategy and to have fought a two-front war. In opposition to all the efforts to melt it into the syncretistic hodge-podge of the Roman Empire—in which, to quote Gibbon's lapidary sentence, "the various modes of worship which prevailed in the Roman world were all considered by the people as equally true; by the philosopher as equally false; and by the magistrate as equally useful"[23]—Christianity had sharpened the precision of its self-defining identity, excluding from its midst those movements that appeared to be blurring the boundaries between the Christian faith and all those other "various modes of worship."

Yet it had also been engaged at the very same time in casting off all those conceptions of its identity that would have restricted it to less than the *oikoumené*, that is to say, the known, civilized world, which must in turn include the entire Roman Empire but may not be confined even to it. One of the most far-reaching implications of the Christian separation from Judaism was this redefinition of identity, for Judaism certainly did have and does have a universal vision: "Are you not like the Ethiopians to me, O people of Israel?" was the word to the prophet (Amos 9:7). In the Roman Empire during the Hellenistic period, moreover, that universal vision was at work interpreting the Jewish faith as a system of belief and worship intended for non-Jews as well. We have the authority of the New Testament itself for the acknowledgement that Jewish leaders were willing to "traverse sea and land to make a single proselyte" (Matt.

23:15), and the evidence of the Greek translation of the Old Testament, the Septuagint, as well as the thought of Philo of Alexandria for the skill and sensitivity with which Hellenistic Judaism was able to pursue the task of carrying the tradition of Israel beyond the borders of Israel. Whether it might have succeeded in that enterprise and for that matter whether the rise of Christianity was responsible for its not having succeeded are questions too important and complex to be considered in this context. The Christian church did in fact inherit from Judaism its catholic vision of "identity plus universality." In the process it rejected attempts to slough off the Jewish Scriptures as well as attempts to retain the Jewish ceremonial law. By taking over the Septuagint and then by allegorizing it, the church laid claim to the Jewish Bible as its own "Old Testament," but by gradually adding a "New Testament" to the "Old," it defined itself by means of a special, indeed a unique, identity. The "mission and expansion of Christianity in the first three centuries"[24] enabled the catholicity of the church to become a public fact just as the Roman Empire was passing into its decline and fall. Or, in Gibbon's double-edged words, "while that great body [of the Roman Empire] was invaded by open violence, or undermined by slow decay, a pure and humble religion gently insinuated itself into the minds of men, grew up in silence and obscurity, derived new vigour from opposition, and finally erected the triumphant banner of the cross on the ruins of the Capitol."[25]

Like the other three "notes of the church," the designation of the church as *apostolic* can be interpreted both as a theological doctrine and as a social statement. As a theological doctrine, it represented the fundamental method of distinguishing between what was legitimate and what was illegitimate in Christian teaching: only that which had "apostolic" sanction, howsoever defined, could claim the loyalty and obedience of believers; all other theories, of which there would inevitably be a great many, were just that—theories—to which individuals or groups were entitled only if and insofar as they did not conflict, either explicitly or implicitly, with the apostolic norm. The three "criteria of apostolic continuity"[26]—apostolic Scripture, apostolic tradition, and apostolic episcopate—interacted with one another to form the standard of Christian truth and, in the most comprehensive sense of the term, the "rule of faith." Conversely, no one of these criteria stood by itself; each had to be related to the other two. Only in later centuries, above all of course in the Reformation of the sixteenth century, did one or another branch of the church disturb that balance, with far-reaching consequences for every article of Christian doctrine.

As is obvious from the presence of the apostolic episcopate within that triad of criteria of apostolicity, the social structure of the church no less than the creed and doctrine of the church was defined by its continuity with the apostles. In the most direct organizational sense, this meant that the bishops of the church laid claim to a succession from the twelve apostles of Christ, transmitted through the laying on of hands and recorded in "bishop lists" for later generations to consult as they sought the credentials of a claimant to episcopal authority. It meant as well that the day-to-day governance of the church lay in the hands of what has come to be called the "monarchical episcopate," from which, through ordination and confirmation, the other forms of church structure were eventually believed to be derived. When a crisis arose, moreover, the precedent of the "apostolic council" described earlier meant that, at the local or regional level, the bishops would form themselves into a legislative body. But as the church became fully "catholic" in a geographical sense, the need arose for such a legislative body that could speak both for and to the universal church. That extension of the "apostolic council" to a position of universal authority created the concept of the "ecumenical council," with "ecumenical" here taking the double meaning of "for the general church as a whole" and "imperial in scope and in authority" (*oikoumené* meaning also, as noted earlier, at least "the Roman Empire").

Therefore it is not a coincidence that the first such "ecumenical council" was convoked by the emperor Constantine soon after his conversion to Christianity. He looked upon his conversion as a sign not of the decline and fall of the Roman Empire, but of its preservation and continuity in the new form of a "Christian empire" with a "Christian capital" at New Rome, Constantinople. Most historians are agreed that he probably saw in the empire-wide distribution of the church and in its system of "apostolic" administrative authority a useful structure for bringing together and holding together a Roman Empire that appeared to him to have become the victim of centripetal social, political, and military forces. And at Nicea he strove to make use of the opportunity. Because of the liturgical and theological prominence of the Nicene Creed, it is easy to forget that the Council of Nicea in 325 legislated on a great variety of matters, many of them primarily social rather than doctrinal: personal and professional qualifications of candidates for the priesthood, conflicts of jurisdiction among bishops, the legitimacy or illegitimacy of military service for Christians, transfers of bishops from one diocese to another, the lending of money at interest. All four "notes" had equipped the ancient church for the tasks that, beginning with the conversion of Constantine and the Council of Nicea, it was about to undertake. Its "social triumph" was at the same time its assumption of these new responsibilities—new for the ancient church and no less new for the Roman Empire. "Decline and fall" for the old empire meant at the same time "rise and triumph" for the new church.

This all but unanimous interpretation of the decline and fall of the Roman Empire and the establishment of the one, holy, catholic, and apostolic church as a "social triumph" may be said to have been the fundamental assumption of medieval culture, both in the Greek East and in the Latin West. But it bears noting that the all but unanimous celebration of the "social triumph of the ancient church" had become considerably less than unanimous well before Gibbon's reconstructionist history. In the summary words of Walter Rauschenbusch,

For centuries before the Reformation, the instinct of Christian men had located the fundamental cause for the corruption of the church. It was a common conviction that the debasement of the church had set in with the "Donation of Constantine," by which the Emperor Constantine was supposed to have conferred large territories and sovereign rights on Pope Sylvester in the fourth century. That had been "the poisoned bone which the devil had thrown and which the church had swallowed." Since then the church has become an antichristian power. Constantly the bolder reformatory spirits taught that the church could be saved only by surrendering its wealth and political power and returning to apostolic poverty, supported only by the free gifts of those who loved her.[27]

The "social triumph of the ancient church" was, by that reading of its history, "the social tragedy of the ancient church." Or, to put the matter the other way around, the clinical judgments about "decline and fall" were now seen as having applied at least as forcefully to the Christian victor as to the Roman vanquished. Whether one accepts such a radical reading both of the history of Rome and of the history of the church or not, it serves at the very least to corroborate the thesis that whenever there is "decline and fall," whether in politics or in economics or in religion, we are, in the phrase of Karl Marx, "reminded of ancient Rome."

CHAPTER 3

The Triumph of
Barbarism and Religion

Edward Gibbon's own familiar description of his *History of the Decline and Fall of the Roman Empire,* formulated in the final chapter of that work, declares: "In the preceding volumes of this History, I have described the triumph of barbarism and religion." Less often quoted but surely no less indicative of his purpose are the sentences that precede and follow this description. "The crowd of writers of every nation," Gibbon's paragraph opens, "who impute the destruction of the Roman monuments to the Goths and the Christians [thus to 'barbarism' and to 'religion'], have neglected to inquire how far they were animated by an hostile principle and how far they possessed the means and the leisure to satiate their enmity." And the second half of the sentence about "barbarism and religion" reads: "and I can only resume, in a few words, their real *or imaginary* connexion with the ruin of ancient Rome."[1] In the final sentence of that chapter, and thus of the entire work, in an epilogue dated 27 June 1787 at Lausanne the author informs his readers: "It was among the ruins of the Capitol that I first conceived the idea of a work which has amused and exercised near twenty years of my life, and which, however inadequate to my own wishes, I finally deliver to the curiosity and candour of the public."[2]

That brief notice of the circumstances under which Gibbon conceived of the *Decline and Fall* was considerably amplified as to historical detail as well as philosophical perspective about two years later, probably in 1789, in one of the successive versions (labeled by one of its several editors, Dero A. Saunders, "Version C") of his *Autobiography:*

In my journal the place and moment of conception are recorded: the fifteenth of October, 1764, in the close of evening, as I sat musing in the church of the Zoccolanti [a reform movement in the Order of Friars Minor, established in 1368], or Franciscan friars, while they were singing vespers in the Temple of Jupiter on the ruins of the Capitol.[3]

In the penultimate draft, dated 1790/1791 and labeled "Version E," that sentence was revised into the form in which it is usually quoted from the definitive editions of the *Autobiography:*

It was at Rome, on the 15th of October 1764, as I sat musing amid the ruins of the Capitol, while the barefooted friars were singing vespers in the temple of Jupiter, that the idea of writing the decline and fall of the city first started to my mind.[4]

He adds the revealing explanatory note that his "original plan was circumscribed to the decay of the city rather than of the empire," as well as the comment, which many an author of a large-scale work of scholarship could repeat, that "though my reading and reflections began to point toward that object, some years elapsed, and several avocations intervened, before I was seriously engaged in the execution of that laborious work."[5]

He remained more or less (first less, and then much more) "seriously engaged" in its execution for almost a quarter of a century. Periodically in the course of its publication, he would pause to survey his narrative and to suggest some tentative conclusions on the basis of the narrative up to that point about the underlying historical factors that helped to explain what he called in the preface "the memorable series of revolutions which, in the course of about thirteen centuries, gradually undermined, and at length destroyed, the fabric of human greatness."[6] It would, therefore, be an unjust and simplistic use of the lapidary phrase "the triumph of barbarism and religion" to ignore these periodic summaries: in addition to those that are no more than extended phrases, such as "the decline of the empire by the expense of blood and treasure, and by the perpetual increase, as well of the taxes as of the military establishment,"[7] two of these amounted to only a concluding paragraph each and another was an introductory projection setting out the "plan of the two last [quarto] Volumes" of the total work; but two others, one at the halfway point and the other at the very end, were small essays on the subject. The development of these summary judgments provides useful insights into the evolution of the *Decline and*

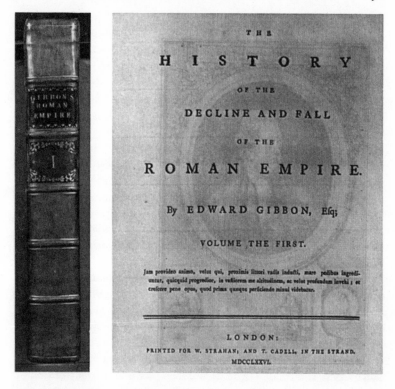

Spine and title page from the first volume of Edward Gibbon's *The History of the Decline and Fall of the Roman Empire*, London, 1776. Photos by E. Bruce Howell, Courtesy of Doheny Library, University of Southern California, Los Angeles.

Fall as a work of historiography and into the maturation of Gibbon's reflection on the subtle problems of historical periodization and historical causation, including the triumph of barbarism and religion. Some of this material will engage us at greater length in later chapters, but it deserves first to be put into the context in which it stands within the work as a total literary entity.

Although there are paragraphs identified as "Conclusion" ending earlier chapters, notably the one at the end of the controversial sixteenth chapter summarizing "a melancholy truth" about Christian intolerance,[8] it was only at the end of the succeeding chapter describing the founding of Constantinople in 330 and the administrative and financial system of Constantine that Gibbon stepped back from his account to pull together some observations that, though not surprising in the light of what he had already said in several *obiter dicta* scattered throughout the preceding chapters, had not appeared in quite so explicit a form up to that point. The subjects of the emperor Constantine recognized "the rage of tyranny, the relaxation of discipline, and the increase of taxes" by which they were being oppressed; nevertheless they "were incapable of discerning the decline of genius and manly virtue, which so far degraded them below the dignity of their ancestors." Yet there were at least "some favourable circumstances which tended to alleviate the misery of their condition," including a temporary delay of "the threatening tempest of the barbarians." As a result, they could still enjoy the "arts of luxury and literature," the "elegant pleasures of society," and a "sense of order and equity, unknown to the despotic governments of the east."[9]

Such a mixture of negative and positive comments marks many of Gibbon's conclusions about the decline and fall. The negative predominate, however, in a similar one-paragraph statement at the end of the thirty-fifth chapter describing the situation a century or so later, after the death of Attila the Hun; it bears the subtitle "Symptoms of the Decay and Ruin of the Roman Government." Once again, the burden of taxes and the inequitable distribution of wealth between the rich and the poor are taken as clear omens of "the downfall of the Western empire." An additional factor, mentioned in only one sentence but portentous in the light of subsequent history, was that "the name of Roman citizens, which had formerly excited the ambition of mankind," was now something that citizens themselves often "abjured and abhorred" and that they were now "compelled . . . to prefer the more simple tyranny of the Barbarians" and flee. The "threatening tempest of the barbarians" mentioned at the end of chapter 17 was now no longer threatening but raging. And yet Gibbon would not assign the primary responsibility for the decline and fall to the invaders. Rather, "if all the Barbarian conquerors had been annihilated in the same hour, their total destruction would not have restored the empire of the West; and, if Rome still survived, she survived the loss of freedom, of virtue, and of honour."[10]

Three chapters later, in the final paragraph of chapter 38, Gibbon declares: "I have now accomplished the laborious narrative of the decline and fall of the Roman empire, from the fortunate age of Trajan and the Antonines to its total extinction in the West about five centuries after the Christian era."[11] There followed an excursus, ten pages long in Bury's edition (judging from the separate numbering of the footnotes not part of the chapter proper), bearing the superscription "General Observations on the Fall of the Roman Empire in the West." In this essay Gibbon enumerated, specifically with reference to the barbarians, three "reflections" (as he called them in introducing them) or "speculations" (as he said after enumerating them) that could perhaps "illustrate the fall of that mighty empire," considerations that also showed what he took to be the differences between that time and the present. "The Romans," he stated in his first thesis, "were ignorant of their danger, and the number of their enemies," whereas he was confident that "such formidable emigrations can no longer issue from the North." A second difference was that "the empire of Rome was firmly established by the singular and perfect coalition of its members," yet at the cost of national independence; but now Europe was fortunately divided into many nations, so that "the abuses of tyranny are restrained by the mutual influence of fear and shame." Finally, although "cold, poverty, and a life of danger and fatigue, fortify the strength and courage of Barbarians," it was comforting to know that now, thanks to the advances of military technology, "Europe is secure from any future irruption of Barbarians; since, before they can conquer, they must cease to be barbarous."[12]

As he opened chapter 48, and with it the last two quarto volumes of the work, Gibbon, having covered "the regular series of the Roman emperors" from the accession of Trajan in 98 C.E. to the death of Heraclius in 641, noted that "five centuries of the decline and fall of the empire have already elapsed," but that "a period of more than eight hundred years still separates me from the term of my labours, the taking of Constantinople by the Turks" in 1453. Fearing that "the patient reader [would not] find an adequate reward of instruction or amusement"[13] if the book were to continue at that pace, he acknowledged that he, too, found it an "ungrateful and melancholy task" to contemplate giving equal time to "a tedious and uniform tale of weakness and misery," the history of the Byzantine Empire. That history was, he complained, one in which "the line of empire . . . recedes on all sides from our view." In this transition from the Roman Empire to the Byzantine Empire, "the

Roman name, the proper subject of our inquiries, is reduced to a narrow corner of Europe, to the lonely suburbs of Constantinople." Nevertheless, he would forge ahead with his account of "the Byzantine annals," incorporating his treatment of the various other Eastern and Western peoples into that framework. The book would conclude with another "triumph," this time neither the triumph of the ancient church nor the triumph of barbarism and religion, but the triumph of Mohammed II and the fall of Constantinople; "and his triumph," Gibbon observed, "annihilates the remnant, the image, the title, of the Roman empire in the East." After that, he would "return from the captivity of the new, to the ruins of ancient, ROME," where his whole enterprise had begun; "and the venerable name, the interesting theme, will shed a ray of glory on the conclusion of my labours."[14]

The most systematic of Gibbon's "reflections" or "speculations" about the decline and fall (also coming to ten pages of text in the Bury edition) came, logically enough, in the concluding chapter. "After a diligent inquiry," it begins, "I can discern four principal causes of the ruin of Rome"; but he specified that he was considering here not the individual events, some of them quite dramatic and even important (such as Alaric's sack of the city), but only those causes "which continued to operate in a period of more than a thousand years." Those causes were: "I. The injuries of time and nature." Here he was referring to the capacity of "the art of man . . . to construct monuments far more permanent than the narrow span of his own existence," such as the pyramids or the Colosseum; "yet these monuments, like [man] himself," Gibbon warns, "are perishable and frail; and in the boundless annals of time, his life and his labours must equally be measured as a fleeting moment." So it had been also with the monuments of Rome. "II. The hostile attacks of the barbarians and Christians." This was the heading under which the words "the triumph of barbarism and religion" appeared, but by the time Gibbon had completed his analysis of these "attacks" their place in the causal scheme had become quite ambiguous. "III. The use and abuse of the materials." Prefacing his examination of this abuse with some observations on the theory of value, Gibbon proceeded to describe the process by which "the edifices of Rome [came to] be considered as a vast and various mine," from which the builders of the Middle Ages drew metal, stone, and works of art. "And, IV. The domestic quarrels of the

Romans." Here Gibbon was referring especially to the centuries in the history of medieval Italy "when every quarrel was decided by the sword and none could trust their lives or properties to the impotence of law," so that "the licentiousness of private war" had replaced law and order.[15]

Although such autopsies reflected the prejudice of the coroner, not only the condition of the victim, Gibbon was, here and throughout the *Decline and Fall,* speaking professedly and deliberately as a historian, and in the *Autobiography* he pondered retrospectively the almost providential character of the forces in his early experience that had made him into one. His formal university schooling was definitely not one of those forces: "To the University of Oxford," he wrote many years later, "I acknowledge no obligation, and she will as cheerfully renounce me for a son as I am willing to disclaim her for a mother." The fourteen months he spent as an undergraduate at Magdalen College were "the most idle and unprofitable of my whole life."[16] Whether or not the experience, at age sixteen, of having "bewildered myself in the errors of the Church of Rome,"[17] helped him to understand the primitive Catholicism of the early Christian centuries depends primarily on one's evaluation of his treatment of those centuries in chapters 15 and 16. One early experience that did contribute to his becoming a historian was his military service, from June 1760 to December 1762, which, he said, made him "an Englishman and a soldier." It also gave him that eye for military formation, military dress, and above all military discipline (or the lack of it) that he then brought repeatedly to his examination of the Roman armies. In this sense, as he put it in his well-known epigram, "The discipline and evolution of a modern battalion gave me a clearer notion of the phalanx and the legions, and the captain of the Hampshire grenadiers (the reader may smile) has not been useless to the historian of the Roman empire."[18] Among ancient historians, perhaps among all historians, Gibbon's ideal was Tacitus, "the first of historians who applied the science of philosophy to the study of facts."[19] From Tacitus as historian he had learned that "wars and the administration of public affairs are the principal subjects of history,"[20] from Tacitus as philosopher that "history, which undertakes to record the transactions of the past, for the instruction of the future, ages, would ill deserve that honourable office, if she condescended to plead the cause of tyrants, or to justify the maxims of persecution."[21]

By far the greatest attention has been paid, in his own time and since, to the two chapters in which Gibbon the historian deals with the first centuries of the church.[22] He even won praise for them from the one man among his contemporaries in the British Isles who most, like Tacitus, combined the philosopher and the historian, David Hume, through whom, "in the present age, Scotland arose to dispute the prize with Italy herself" about who were the best historians in modern languages.[23] Six months before his own death in August 1776, Hume wrote Gibbon a cordial letter congratulating him on the *Decline and Fall* and singling out those two chapters for special comment.[24] At the opposite end of British religious philosophy, John Henry Newman observed in 1845: "It is melancholy to say it, but the chief, perhaps the only English writer who has any claim to be considered an ecclesiastical historian is the unbeliever Gibbon."[25] Gibbon tells us in his *Autobiography* that while he wrote the first chapter of the *Decline and Fall* three times and the second and third chapters twice, he did the fifteenth and sixteenth four times in all, first in the original composition and then in "three successive revisals," which reduced them "from a large volume to their present size."[26] When he went on to add that "they might still be compressed without any loss of facts or sentiments," he did not mean that he would have been willing to excise any of the statements about Christian history that his contemporaries found the most offensive.

What they found offensive about these chapters, apart from certain matters of tone and taste, was also what Gibbon himself found least susceptible to "revisal," the treatment of ecclesiastical history by the same methods and criteria of evidence that pertained to every other kind of history. Gibbon put it in his own unmistakable manner already in the second paragraph of his fifteenth chapter:

The theologian may indulge the pleasing task of describing Religion as she descended from Heaven, arrayed in her native purity. A more melancholy duty is imposed on the historian. He must discover the inevitable mixture of error and corruption which she contracted in a long residence upon earth, among a weak and degenerate race of beings.[27]

Quite apart from the question of whether in the judgment of Edward Gibbon or of anyone else there could ever be a theologian who in fact carried out that "pleasing task," the distinction meant that neither the subject matter nor the source materials of early Christianity had any privileged character. When he said in an earlier discussion of the fourth century that "the impartial historian" was "obliged to extract truth from satire as well as from panegyric,"[28] he was referring to Christian panegyric in honor of Constantine at least as much as to pagan panegyric in honor of Diocletian. And when he spoke of disentangling history from fable or from poetry, he meant above all the fables and the poetry of the church.[29] Nor did Gibbon emulate the ecclesiastical historians of his time (and not only of his time) in applying that critical method to the fourth century and then the third and then the second, but suddenly stopping at the sacred boundaries of the first, though he was circumspect about applying it to the New Testament and even to the Gospels— circumspect to the point of being arch.

From the literally hundreds of examples, let two suffice. One appears in a footnote intended to identify "Apollonius the philosopher": "Apollonius of Tyana was born about the same time as Jesus Christ. His life *(that of the former)* is related in so fabulous a manner by his disciples, that we are at a loss to discover whether he was a sage, an impostor, or a fanatic."[30] Now Gibbon was certainly an adept enough English stylist to avoid writing himself into an ambiguity that made such a parenthetical explanation necessary—unless the ambiguity was intentional. In the other example, which is better known but so representative that despite its length it deserves to be quoted in full, Gibbon's coyness nearly overreached itself. Professing surprise at pagan indifference to the evidences of the apologists for the credibility of the Christian message, he asks:

But how shall we excuse the supine inattention of the Pagan and philosophic world to those evidences which were presented by the hand of Omnipotence, not to their reason, but to their senses? During the age of Christ, of his apostles, and of their first disciples, the doctrine which they preached was confirmed by innumerable prodigies. The lame walked, the blind saw, the sick were healed, the dead were raised, daemons were expelled, and the laws of Nature were frequently suspended for the benefit of the church. But the sages of Greece and Rome turned aside from the awful spectacle, and, pursuing the ordinary occupations of life and study, appeared unconscious of any alterations in the moral or physical government of the world. Under the reign of Tiberius [at noon on Good Friday], the whole earth, or at least a celebrated province of the Roman empire, was involved in a praeternatural darkness of three hours. Even this miraculous event, which ought to have excited the wonder, the curiosity, and the devotion of mankind, passed without notice in an age of science and history.[31]

Such statements explain what Gibbon meant when he recalled that "from the *Provincial Letters* of Pascal, which almost every year I have perused with new pleasure, I learned to manage the weapon of grave and temperate irony, even on subjects of ecclesiastical solemnity."[32]

The same critics who professed to be shocked at Gibbon's ironic and rationalistic treatment of sacred history—and some who were not shocked at it—were offended by the style of his treatment of sex. Professing surprise at this "reproach of indecency [that] has been loudly echoed by the rigid censors of morals," Gibbon replied: "My English text is chaste, and all licentious passages are left in the obscurity of a learned language. 'Le Latin dans se mots brave l'honnêteté.'"[33] That means of protecting the innocent reader (or of provoking the innocent reader into studying the classics) adapted the precedent of Tillemont, who in his treatment of Cyril of Alexandria "has thrown his virtues into the text, and his faults into the notes, in decent obscurity."[34] It is illustrated already in the Latin passages quoted repeatedly in the footnotes of the early chapters of the *Decline and Fall,* particularly in discussing male sexual excesses of various kinds.[35] But the most lurid passages and the ones that appear to have been the most prominent in the critiques appeared in the fortieth chapter, dealing with the emperor Justinian and with "the woman whom he loved, the famous Theodora, whose strange elevation cannot be applauded as the triumph of female virtue . . . the prostitute who, in the presence of innumerable spectators, had polluted the theatre of Constantinople."[36] Gibbon's account of Theodora is based on the *Secret History* of "the historian Procopius," to whom he had earlier attributed "a ray of human prudence or celestial wisdom,"[37] commodities that were, Gibbon was sure, in even shorter supply among the Byzantines than they had been among the Romans. In his scholarly bibliographical appendix on Procopius, Bury has correctly noted that "it was recognized by Gibbon, and has been confirmed by later investigations, that in the history of events previous to his own times Procopius is untrustworthy." Bury adds that "his description of the profligacy of Theodora only proves his familiarity with the pornography of the stews of Constantinople; but it rests on the solid fact that the youth of Theodora was disreputable."[38] Gibbon exploited the decent obscurity of the learned language in which that pornography appeared, and there may be more Greek in chapter 40 than in almost any other chapter.[39] Apart from an undeniable prurience, another motivation may also have been Gibbon's view of the history of the Byzantine Empire, for which Theodora's profligacy was a particularly unsavory example.

By writing (to use his own words) as a "historian" rather than as a "theologian," by subjecting the history of the church to the same methodological criteria that pertained to all other chapters of history, and by speaking candidly about matters that were often regarded as indecent for mixed company, Gibbon was deliberately setting his work apart from the piety and orthodoxy of the apologists who had treated this subject matter before him and who, of course, went on treating it in their own fashion long after him, as the spate of Victorian novels like Bulwer-Lytton's *The Last Days of Pompeii,* Newman's *Callista,* Kingsley's *Hypatia,* and Wallace's *Ben Hur* will attest. But in addition to viewing his *Decline and Fall of the Roman Empire* in the setting of eighteenth-century rationalism and Enlightenment historiography, for both of which it is a major primary document, we need to understand it against the background of the conventional wisdom about the decline and fall that the eighteenth century had inherited from early and medieval Christian sources. In the chapters that follow, therefore, we shall turn to the explicit and implicit contrasts between that conventional wisdom, for which Jerome, Eusebius-Socrates-Sozomen, and Augustine served as spokesmen, and Gibbon's *Decline and Fall,* as those contrasts are represented by the fundamental contrast between "the social triumph of the ancient church" and "the triumph of barbarism and religion" (even though the former received that precise formulation only after Gibbon, but not, it would seem, in conscious response to Gibbon).

Gibbon's memoir of the visit to the Capitol on 15 October 1764, when, amid the chants of the Franciscan friars, he conceived the idea of writing the *Decline and Fall,* has its counterpart in a later memoir—with the same self-consciousness and the same touch of pomposity as the first:

I have presumed to mark the moment of conception; I shall now commemorate the hour of my final deliverance. It was on the day, or rather, night, of the 27th of June 1787, between the hours of eleven and twelve, that I wrote the last lines of the last page in a summerhouse in my garden. . . . I will not dissemble the first emotions of joy on recovery of my freedom, and perhaps the establishment of my fame. But my pride was soon humbled, and a sober melancholy was spread over my mind, by the idea that I had taken an everlasting leave of an old and agreeable companion, and that whatsoever might be the future fate of my *History,* the life of the historian must be short and precarious.⁴⁰

"Books have their special fates [*Habent sua fata libelli*]," the proverbial saying of Terentianus Maurus declared, but Gibbon need not have worried about the "future fate" of his *History.* It has been criticized from Gibbon's time to our own. It has also been bowdlerized, and that by none less than Dr. Thomas Bowdler himself, who in 1825 published a five-volume edition "adapted to the use of families and young persons," in which he had expunged "the indecent expressions and all allusions of an improper tendency." And yet Gibbon's work has remained in print for two centuries. Translations into other languages, including German and Russian, have extended its influence, as have abridgements in its own language. The bicentennial of its first volume in 1976 evoked a number of scholarly and commemorative responses, and the bicentennial of its final volume in 1988 will probably do the same.

Evelyn Waugh, the author of a novel entitled *Decline and Fall,* paid Gibbon the kind of oblique compliment that he himself was fond of paying his predecessors. In another of Waugh's novels, one about the mother of the emperor Constantine (in which Helena advises her son, "Keep out of history, Constantine"), Lactantius, the Christian historian of persecution and martyrdom, appears as a character. He meets with Helena in the presence of "an Indian ape, the recent expensive present of a visiting diplomat." Waugh continues, with Lactantius speaking:

"You see it is equally possible to give the right form to the wrong thing, and the wrong form to the right thing. Suppose that in years to come, when the Church's troubles seem to be over, there should come an apostate of my own trade, a false historian, with the mind of Cicero or Tacitus and the soul of an animal," and he nodded toward the gibbon who fretted his golden chair and chattered for fruit. "A man like that might make it his business to write down the martyrs and excuse the persecutors. He might be refuted again and again but what he wrote would remain in people's minds when the refutations were quite forgotten. That is what style does— it has the Egyptian secret of the embalmers."⁴¹

Thus, like the only work on the subject of the fall of Rome with which it may properly be compared, Augustine's *City of God* (much as they would both dislike the comparison), Gibbon's *Decline and Fall* has continued to define the issues for its adversaries no less than for its admirers. And that is for any book the happiest of fates.

Part Two

THE LESSONS OF HISTORY

The pilgrims of the North [in] their rude enthusiasm
. . . broke forth in a sublime proverbial expression,
which is recorded in the eighth century, in the fragments of the venerable Bede: "As long as the Coliseum stands, Rome shall stand; when the Coliseum
falls, Rome will fall; when Rome falls, the world will
fall."

CHAPTER 4

History as Divine Apocalypse

In the course of his summary of what he took to be the five principal "secondary causes" for the success of Christianity—the primary cause, "that it was owing to the convincing evidence of the doctrine itself, and to the ruling providence of its great Author," having been, despite its (in his ironic words) "obvious but satisfactory" force, declared to be outside the province of the historian—Gibbon came to a discussion, under the second cause, "The doctrine of a future life," of what he called "an opinion which, however it may deserve respect for its usefulness and antiquity, has not been found agreeable to experience," namely, "that the end of the world and the kingdom of Heaven were at hand," with which "the ancient and popular doctrine of the Millennium was intimately connected." A central element of that doctrine was "the destruction of the mystic Babylon," the "epithet . . . applied to the city and to the empire of Rome." Although there were others who also thought that the end of the world might be near, the Christian

. . . expected it with terror and confidence, as a certain and approaching event; and, as his mind was perpetually filled with the solemn idea, he considered every disaster that happened to the empire as an infallible symptom of an expiring world.[1]

Therefore the way of celebrating the social triumph of the early church that made itself the most evident at the time of the fall of Rome was a resurgence of Christian belief in "apocalypse now," albeit in a chastened form.

The most eloquent spokesman for this chastened apocalypticism, with his capacity for "vehement invectives,"[2] was Jerome, Christian humanist, translator of the Bible into Latin, and probably the greatest scholar of the early Christian centuries (his only possible rival for that title might be Origen). His words are no less eloquent and poignant for their being quite familiar. "For days and nights," Jerome recalled as he wrote the preface to his *Commentary on Ezekiel*, "I could think of nothing but the universal safety." This was true at both the personal and the civic level. "When my friends were captured," he continued, "I could only imagine myself a captive too." But something greater than any individual was at stake; for "when the brightest light of the world was extinguished, when the very head of the Roman empire was severed, the entire world perished in a single city [*in una urbe totus orbis interiit*]."[3] Later in the same commentary he exclaimed: "Who could believe that after being raised up by victories over the whole world, Rome should come crashing down, and become at once the mother and the grave of her peoples!"[4] In a subsequent description of the time when he wrote those words, Jerome said in a letter:

When I began to dictate [the *Commentary on Ezekiel*], I was so confounded by the havoc wrought in the West and above all by the sack of Rome [at the hands of Alaric in 410] that, as the common saying has it, I forgot even my own name. Long did I remain silent, knowing that it was a time to weep.[5]

And again in the next letter: "My voice sticks in my throat; and, as I dictate, sobs choke my utterance. The City which had taken the world was itself taken."[6] He recalled not only the prophecies of Scripture, but the hexameter of Virgil about the fall of Troy, expressing what Gordon Williams has called "an agony so great that mere words cannot do it justice":[7]

> Urbs antiqua ruit, multos dominata per annos.
> [The ancient city falls, after dominion
> Many long years.][8]

And yet again in the very next letter: "The world is sinking into ruins. . . . The renowned city, the capital of the Roman empire, is swallowed up in one tremendous fire; and there is no part of the earth where Romans are not in exile."[9]

In such sentiments at the sack of Rome, which could easily be multiplied from the six essay-epistles that Jerome devoted to this theme between 407 and 414,[10] he was speaking in the accents of apocalypse. Already in an earlier letter dated 396 C.E., he had said:

"I shudder when I think of the catastrophes of our time," and he had quoted from the same section of the *Aeneid:*

> Crudelis ubique
> luctus, ubique pavor et plurima mortis imago.
> [Grief everywhere,
> Everywhere terror, and all shapes of death.][11]

Going on from Virgil, he admonished his readers: "The Roman world is falling, and yet we are holding up our heads instead of bowing them down!" Thus already in the closing years of the fourth century (and before the barbarian armies had marched to the gates of the Eternal City), Jerome believed himself to be witnessing a wave of assassinations and executions combined with invasions, wars, and rumors of wars that had created a social and political situation at which even Thucydides and Sallust would be struck dumb. And he took the occasion of the death of a friend's son to warn of apocalypse now. Once again, he went beyond the individual to the civic dimension, first consoling his friend personally and then speaking of history in general. "While forbidding you to weep for one dead man," he noted near the conclusion, "I have myself been mourning the dead of the whole world."[12]

That apocalyptic set of mind received further stimulation from the events of the first decade of the fifth century. This was the time when, in Gibbon's description, "the emperor Honorius was distinguished, above his subjects, by the pre-eminence of fear, as well as of rank." And so, at "the sound of war," the emperor's "timid counsellors" urged him to flee. The exception was Stilicho, general of the Roman army, who, whatever his complicity in one or another "crime" may have been,[13] "alone had courage and authority to resist this disgraceful measure, which would have abandoned Rome and Italy to the Barbarians."[14] His courage and authority moved Stilicho, however, to propose that the senate of Rome award a subsidy to Alaric, king of the Goths, and the proposal "obtained, after a warm debate, the reluctant approbation of the senate."[15] It was an approbation that Jerome decidedly did not share. This "half-barbarian traitor," he complained—alluding to the circumstance that, in Gibbon's words, "the general who so long commanded the armies of Rome was descended [on his father's side] from the savage and perfidious race of the Vandals"[16]—"has used our money to arm our enemies against us."[17] Once again he quoted Virgil on the "crimes [*scelera*]" and the "punishments [*poenae*]" of the time,[18] but once again he also quoted Scripture.

Contemporary events were prompting Jerome to turn to biblical prophecy. The first two of the three epistles attributed in the New Testament to the apostle John had spoken several times about "the Antichrist," which probably means "one in place of [the root meaning of *anti* in Greek] Christ": there were "many Antichrists," but *the* Antichrist was coming, "the deceiver and the Antichrist" (1 John 2:18, 2:22, 4:3; 2 John 7). Additional details about the portrait—and eventually, so it was believed, about the identity—of the Antichrist were supplied in the second chapter of the Second Epistle to the Thessalonians, which has been called "possibly the earliest Christian belief in an antichrist combined with a pseudo Christ."[19] There the apostle Paul, or someone writing in his name, had announced: "The mystery of iniquity is already at work. Only let the one who is now restraining it do so until he is out of the way" (2 Thess. 2:7). This prophecy meant that "the one who is now restraining it" would begin to lose his hold, thus making it possible for someone called "the man of sin, the son of perdition" to appear; that Pauline figure was early equated with the "Antichrist" of John. "The one who is now restraining it is removed," Jerome wrote in 409, not long before Alaric's sack of Rome, "and yet we do not realize that Antichrist is near. Yes, Antichrist is near, whom the Lord Jesus Christ 'shall consume with the spirit of his mouth [and destroy with the brilliance of his advent].' "[20] And in two of his biblical commentaries he made the identification that "the one who is now restraining it" referred to the Roman Empire, whose continuance was all that stood between the human race and the end of the world.[21]

The first theologian of the Latin West, "the stern Tertullian" and "the zealous African" as Gibbon calls him,[22] had already come out in favor of this interpretation.[23] "Antichrist," he asserted, was already "now close at hand."[24] He argued elsewhere that the "man of sin" and "son of perdition" in 2 Thessalonians was indeed identical with the "Antichrist" of the Johannine Epistles.[25] And in yet another treatise he quoted the formula "the one who is now restraining it" from 2 Thessalonians, explaining: "What obstacle is there [to the coming of the man of sin, the son of perdition] but the Roman state, the falling away of which . . . shall introduce Antichrist?"[26] The most complete statement of Tertullian's understanding of the place of Rome in the divine economy came in what Gibbon calls "the vehement assertions" of his *Apology,* [27] which Johannes Quasten has correctly characterized as "the most important of all Tertullian's works."[28] This was a defense of the Christians against the repeated charge that by their transcendent loyalty to Christ as Lord they must be guilty of disloyalty to Caesar and to the Roman Empire. On the contrary, Tertullian insisted, the Christians prayed "in behalf of the emperors, nay, for the complete stability of the empire, and for Roman interests in general." And the reason was this: "We know that a mighty shock impending over the whole earth—in fact, the very end of all things, threatening dreadful woes—is being retarded only by the continued existence of the Roman Empire."[29] By their prayers, then, the Christians were not only not jeopardizing the empire; they were "lending aid to Rome's duration" and thus manifesting their loyalty in the best way they knew how.

In a later chapter of the same work Tertullian elaborated on this defense of Christian prayer as a loyal support rather than a political threat to the Roman Empire. Giving his pagan readers (as well as modern scholars, who are hard pressed for every scrap of information they can glean about early Christian liturgy) a glimpse into the practices of worship in the late second century, he spoke of the reading of Scripture in Christian assemblies for its contemporary message, "if anything in the nature of the times bids us look to the future or open our eyes to facts." But in recounting, for the benefit of the Roman magistrates to whom he was addressing his defense, the specific content of Christian public prayer as it pertained to Rome, he itemized the petitions of the liturgy: "We pray also for the emperors, for their ministers, and for those in authority, for the security of the world, for peace on earth—for the postponement of the end."[30] This surprising final phrase, "We pray for the postponement of the end," for which we do not possess any corroboration in the few liturgical sources that have come down from this period, seems almost to suggest a formal prayer. Whether it does or not, it stands in striking contrast to what does seem to have been a formal prayer combined with a formal promise in the next to the last verse of the last chapter of the last book of the Christian Bible: "He who testifies to these things says, 'Surely I am coming soon.' Amen. Come, Lord Jesus" (Rev. 22:20). And it affords a highly significant insight into the attitude of at least this one Christian thinker to the relation between the continuance of the Roman Empire and its decline and fall.

Speaking in a later work, written in 212 or so to the Roman

proconsul of Africa, Tertullian explained again what was at work in these prayers for the emperor, addressed, as he said, "to our God and his." He noted that a Christian was obliged to desire and to pray for the well-being both of the emperor himself and of "the empire over which he reigns, as long as the world shall stand." And the reason for this was that "for so long as [the world shall stand] shall Rome continue."[31] It was an elaboration of those very words that eventually found its way into what Gibbon quotes as "a sublime proverbial expression" in the final chapter of the *Decline and Fall*.[32] The proverb came from one "Caractacus" and was quoted by the Venerable Bede, who had in so many ways "scattered some rays of light over the darkness of the eighth century" of British history;[33] Gibbon surmised that it "must be ascribed to the Anglo-Saxon pilgrims who visited Rome before the year 735," since it was unlikely "that our venerable monk ever passed the sea" to have learned it directly. Whatever its source and its transmission, the proverb summarized well the pagan belief in Rome as *Roma aeterna*, but also the Christian belief that the Roman Empire was "the one who is now restraining" the coming of Antichrist and the end: *"Quamdiu stabit Colyseus, stabit et Roma; quando cadet Colyseus, cadet Roma; quando cadet Roma, cadet et mundus* (As long as the Coliseum stands, Rome shall stand; when the Coliseum falls, Rome will fall; when Rome falls, the world will fall)." Thus Tertullian's conviction that the city of Rome was destined to stand as long as the world stood became the common property of Christians in the first four centuries.

In the form that it was to take in Jerome, however, that conviction meant that the awesome events associated with the sack of the city of Rome by Alaric in 410 could not evoke a simple recitation of the gleeful cry over the fall of Rome that appears in what Gibbon calls "a mysterious prophecy, which still forms a part of the sacred canon, but which . . . has very narrowly escaped the proscription of the church,"[34] the Book of Revelation: "Fallen is Babylon, is fallen, Babylon, the great, the Mother of harlots and abominations of the earth" (Rev. 14:8; 17:5). Jerome had written an early letter in 382 on behalf of a mother and daughter, Paula and Eustochium, who were living in the convent at Bethlehem, to Marcella, a Christian woman in Rome. In it he had urged Marcella to leave Rome and to join Paula and Eustochium in Palestine. Contrasting the holy places associated with the birth of Christ and the unholy places of pagan

Rome, he urged her: "Read the Apocalypse of John, and consider what is sung therein about the woman arrayed in purple . . . and about the end of Babylon [meaning Rome]. 'Come out of her, my people,' so the Lord says, 'that ye be not partakers of her sins.' " He was prepared to acknowledge that things had changed in Rome, now that "Rome has a holy church, trophies of apostles and martyrs, a true confession of Christ, the faith has been preached there by an apostle, [and] the name of Christian is daily exalted higher and higher."[35] But the cultural allurements and social pressures of Rome made it far too distracting a place for the practice of the Christian ascetic life, to which they were inviting Marcella.

Nevertheless, Marcella did not accept the invitation, but remained to practice a life of Christian faith and dedication in Rome. When the Goths sacked the city in 410, in Gibbon's words, "Marcella, a Roman lady, equally respectable for her rank, her age, and her piety, was thrown to the ground, and cruelly beaten and whipped";[36] and she died a martyr's death shortly thereafter. It was the presence in Rome of Marcella and of other fellow Christians that profoundly mitigated any apocalyptic glee that Jerome might have felt or expressed over the fall of the city. From her letters to him we know of her interest in biblical scholarship, some of it pertaining to minute questions of scriptural philology and some of it to larger issues of exegesis. A person of considerable family fortune, she created what has to be called a "Christian salon" at her palace in Rome, where the Christian faith replaced gossip and skepticism as the subject of conversation. Jerome wrote a miniature biography of this remarkable woman[37] as a tribute to the service that she had rendered to the twin causes of Christian asceticism and Christian orthodoxy, but she would certainly deserve a modern biography as well. Thus the Rome that was under siege and threat from Alaric's Goths was, in an increasingly powerful sense, a Christian city. "In Rome itself," said Jerome epigrammatically, "paganism is left in solitude."[38] It is significant that not only in the epistolary biography devoted to Marcella, but in most of the other letters cited earlier, Jerome was speaking about sisters and brothers in the faith who had been caught in the catastrophe of the city.

The restraint on a simplistic recitation of apocalypse had another source as well, one that was no less telling. Not only was Rome a Christian city by now, but Jerome was a Roman. To be sure, he was not a Roman by birth. Like the emperor Constantine before him,

who was born at Naissus (now called Nis), and the emperor Justinian after him, who was born in Illyricum (probably of Slavic
parents), Jerome was a native of what is today Yugoslavia. He was
born in a place called "Stridon," part of Dalmatia. As his principal
recent biographer, J. N. D. Kelly, says, "persistent, if unavailing
efforts have . . . been made to discover [Stridon], practically all the
suggestions advanced being in fact little more than guesses."[39] The
Dalmatian birthplace of Jerome was sufficient, however, to give Jan
Hus, the Czech reformer, the justification to refer to him as "that
Slav" and to provide the basis for a medieval and Renaissance
legend according to which Jerome had translated the Bible not only
into Latin, but into some early Slavic tongue. Yet Jerome was a
Roman by the far deeper ties of language and of culture. Just as
Augustine occasionally recalled a few words of what he called
"Punic" from North Africa[40] even though "it is most unlikely that
Augustine spoke anything but Latin,"[41] so also the occasional Dalmatian word in Jerome, such as the use of *sabaium* as the name for
a regional beer,[42] simply goes to prove just how Roman he was, for
he referred to Dalmatian as "a barbarous native language." Jerome's
own language was Latin (although he also knew Greek and, almost
alone among early Christian fathers, Hebrew as well). He was, as
classicists sometimes need to be reminded, the man through whose
rendition of the Bible Latin was to achieve a wider circulation in
both time and space than it had through all the previous writers of
the language put together.

Nor was it only that Jerome spoke and wrote Latin; he lived and
breathed in the atmosphere of Latin literature. We have noted earlier how he would interweave the apocalyptic language of Scripture
about the decline and fall of Rome with the apocalyptic lines of
Virgil's *Aeneid* about the fall of Troy. This is all the more intriguing
in the light of his own having disparaged, in a letter addressed to
the great Latin Christian poet Paulinus of Nola, any attempt to
claim Virgil's *Fourth Eclogue,* with its language about the miraculous
birth of the child through whom heaven and earth would be transformed, as a kind of pagan messianic prophecy. Jerome dismissed
such a reading of the *Fourth Eclogue* as "puerile."[43] By contrast,
Augustine in the *City of God* was much more prepared to grant that
"it is of [Christ] that the most famous poet speaks, poetically indeed."[44] As he put it elsewhere, "it was not to anyone else but
Christ the Lord that the human race" had addressed the lines of the

Fourth Eclogue. [45] The best-known of all of Jerome's references to Latin literature is probably his account of a dream he had while ill.[46] He was dragged before the judgment seat of God and asked to give an account of who he was. "I am a Christian," he replied. But the divine Judge contradicted him, saying: "You are a liar. You are a Ciceronian, not a Christian! For 'where your treasure is, there will your heart be also.' " And Jerome took an oath: "O Lord, if ever I possess or read secular writings [anymore], I have denied thee."[47] As one scholar has observed, this account "has won more emphasis than it really deserves; moreover, in later years he himself made very light of the dream."[48] Whatever else the dream and the vow may mean, the quotations from Virgil's *Aeneid* in Jerome's responses to the fall of Rome prove that they must not be taken to mean a total break with the Latin heritage: he knew many of these texts by heart and did not need to read them anymore.

Thus the fall of Cicero's city to the Gothic barbarians was for Jerome no less than for his pagan contemporaries a tragedy of major proportions, one to which he responded in the language of Christian and of Virgilian apocalypse. Even in his apocalyptic denunciation of Rome as Babylon the harlot addressed to Marcella in 386, he had been forced to admit that Rome had changed during the preceding century.[49] About seven years later, around 393, Jerome composed a polemical treatise *Against Jovinian,* which was a spirited defense of the ascetic doctrine of virginity and celibacy against the effort to interpret the married life of Christians as not inferior in any way to the life of celibates. Jerome based his case for sexual abstinence at least partly on the need to draw a sharper moral distinction between the followers of Christ and the children of this world as they were visible in the Roman society of the time. He sent the treatise to Rome from his monastery in Bethlehem, and, as Kelly observes, "its publication marked the reopening at last of relations between him and the west, particularly the western capital."[50]

Against Jovinian also included in its peroration an apostrophe to Rome. It was a further development of the interpretation, or reinterpretation, of the city of Rome that he had set forth to Marcella. "I will now address myself to you, great Rome," Jerome said. Rome had, he continued, "with the confession of Christ blotted out the blasphemy written on [her] forehead." Now she was truly "the city of the apostle's praises." The Capitol was in ruins and the temple of Jupiter had collapsed, but the state of the Capitol and of the temple of Jupiter meant to Jerome the exact opposite of what they were to mean to Gibbon as he "sat musing." As the example of the city of Nineveh in the days of the prophet Jonah had demonstrated, Rome could "escape the curse wherewith the Savior threatened you in the Apocalypse." And by her confession of the name of Christ she could become, and indeed she had become, "mighty city, mistress-city of the world" again.[51]

In Jerome's apocalyptic philosophy of history, therefore, Rome had indeed declined and fallen, but Rome had also been transformed into the Christian city—still on the Tiber, but presided over by Damasus the pope rather than by the pagan Caesar. And he transferred to Christian Rome the loyalty and the mystique that had previously been attached to pagan Rome. The Roman title "supreme pontiff" was a symbol of the transfer. As Gibbon pointed out, "the title, the ensigns, the prerogatives of SUPREME PONTIFF, which had been instituted by Numa, and assumed by Augustus, were accepted, without hesitation, by seven Christian emperors." It was only in a footnote to that statement that he added: "The assertion of Zosimus that Gratian [the Catholic emperor in 379] was the first who refused the pontifical robe is confirmed beyond a doubt; and the murmurs of bigotry, on that subject, are almost silenced."[52] Soon thereafter—certainly by the time of Pope Leo I at the middle of the fifth century and conceivably even earlier—the title passed to Christian usage for the pope (and occasionally for other prelates). Pagan Rome had fallen; Christian Rome had arisen. It was no longer the old Rome of the Caesars but had become instead the new Rome of the popes and of intellectuals and martyrs like Marcella.

CHAPTER 5

The Register of Human Follies, Crimes, and Misfortunes

To a mind like Jerome's, saturated with imagery from the book of the prophet Ezekiel and from the Apocalypse of Saint John the Divine, the ominous dispatches coming from Rome to Bethlehem could only mean divine apocalypse, the signs of the beginning of the end prophesied in the Gospels and expected in each Christian generation since the first. Without in any way mitigating the human responsibility for the moral consequences of sin and stupidity—even when he was asserting the doctrine of original sin and therefore the inevitability of violations against the law of God, he insisted that sin was due "not to the fault of our nature and creation, but to the frailty and fickleness of human will, which varies from moment to moment"[1]—Jerome looked for the ultimate explanation of historical upheavals like the fall of Rome in the constancy of divine will rather than the fickleness of human will. The lesson of history was that God reigned over the world and that regardless of human vice or virtue his will would be done on earth as it is in heaven.

To a mind like Gibbon's, by contrast, the intentions of the will of God in human history were by no means as clear, and he left that "pleasing task" to others. His "more melancholy duty" as a historian was to "discover the inevitable mixture of error and corruption" that had made itself manifest in human history. "Inevitable" as it was, that mixture was present throughout history, even and especially in the history of the church, as he lost very few opportunities to point out. Yet for the primary business of his *Decline and Fall*, it served a function as a lesson of history, perhaps even as *the* lesson of history, or at any rate of this history of revolution and change. Not only because he is such a master of English prose with such a nice sensitivity to the nuances of discrimination among synonyms, but because his *History of the Decline and Fall of the Roman Empire* makes him a world authority on revolution and change, the opening paragraph of Gibbon's closing chapter was selected to provide the illustrative quotation for the particular meaning of *vicissitude* among various words for "change" in a modern dictionary of synonyms:

More often it is applied to a sweeping and unpredictable change that overturns what has been and so has the character of a revolution or an upheaval: "the place and the object gave ample scope for moralizing on the *vicissitudes* of fortune, which spares neither man nor the proudest of his works, which buries empires and cities in a common grave."[2]

Such observations are sprinkled across all the chapters of the work, but one of the best-known, most characteristic, and most comprehensive appears in his comments on "the two Antonines, [who] governed the Roman world forty-two years [138–180] with the same invariable spirit of wisdom and virtue." Believing as he did that the age of the Antonines was the era that, "if a man were called to fix the period in the history of the world during which the condition of the human race was most happy and prosperous, he would, without hesitation, name," he was moved to describe the emperorship of the elder of the two, Antoninus Pius (138–161), with a memorable epigram: "His reign is marked by the rare advantage of furnishing very few materials for history; which is, indeed, little more than the register of the crimes, follies, and misfortunes of mankind."[3] Each of those three terms occurs repeatedly in the *Decline and Fall;* and since they do not always appear together, nor always in the same order,[4] it seems justifiable to reverse the order here and to draw a somewhat finer distinction among the three than Gibbon himself sometimes does.[5]

Although Gibbon's naturalism would not permit him except in irony to characterize the many portents in earth and sky that form part of his narrative as supernatural occasions when "the tides of ocean and the course of the planets were suspended,"[6] he did pay continuing attention to them as misfortunes that significantly affected the course of Roman history. One of the givens that repeatedly acted as a determining force in history was climate. Thus it was for him "more natural" to attribute the "weakness of his eyes" from which Diocletian's immediate predecessor, Numerianus, suffered to "the heat of the climate" in Persia than to "incessant weeping for his father's death," as the *Augustan History* did.[7] Elsewhere he identified the "climate of Asia [Minor]" as well as its "manners" as the reason for the "servile indolence imposed on" most women there, with the singular exception of "Zenobia, the celebrated queen of Palmyra and the East"; and he blamed "the heat of the climate" at least in part for the "libidinous complexion" of the Arabs.[8] Perhaps the most systematic consideration of the historic role of climate comes at the beginning of his chapter introducing the Germans to his narrative, since climate so obviously differentiated the North out of which they came from the South to which they came. Citing the opinion of "some ingenious writers," including David Hume, "that Europe was much colder formerly than it is at present," resembling modern Canada rather than modern Europe, he went on to assess the influence of climate on "these hardy children of the North," which was, he suggested, "difficult to ascertain, and easy to exaggerate." Yet he was prepared to accept the hypothesis that "the keen air of Germany . . . gave them a kind of strength better adapted to violent exertions than to patient labour, and inspired them with constitutional bravery, which is the result of nerves and spirits." Notwithstanding the advantage that this difference of climate gave the Germans when they were fighting in their native regions, the history of the Roman army proved that "the Romans made war in all climates, and by their excellent discipline were in a great measure preserved in health and vigour." Gibbon could not restrain himself from adding: "It may be remarked that man is the only animal which can live and multiply in every country from the equator to the poles. The hog seems to approach the nearest to our species in that privilege."[9] Returning to this entire question toward the end of his narrative, Gibbon was still skeptical, referring to "the climate (whatsoever may be its influence)."[10]

Beyond climate as such, geography frequently made a difference in historical events. Although the Romans did manage to make war in all climates, one of their defeats was caused by their attempting to do so on "a smooth and barren surface of sandy desert, without a hillock, without a tree, and without a spring of fresh water."[11] On the other hand, "the morasses that surrounded the town [of Ravenna] were sufficient to prevent the approach" of a hostile army.[12] It is not surprising that the sea should have been the most prominent among the geographical features that interested this Englishman, despite his having been in the army as "captain of the Hampshire grenadiers" rather than in the British navy and despite the "feeble armament" of the sea arm in the grand strategy of the Romans by contrast with "the formidable fleets which were equipped and maintained by the republic of Athens during the Peloponnesian war."[13] Because of that contrast Gibbon paid special attention to the advantages that the sea brought to Rome's enemies, when "the example of [the Franks'] success, instructing their countrymen to conceive the advantages, and to despise the dangers, of the sea, pointed out to their enterprising spirit a new road to wealth and glory."[14] Above all, Britannia would learn to rule the waves; and, with a self-deprecating question in a footnote about whether "in the beginning of the fourth century England deserved *all* these commendations," Gibbon took the episode of the usurper Marcus Aurelius Carausius, who held power in Britain from 286 to 293, to describe how "under his command, Britain, destined in a future age to obtain the empire of the sea, already assumed its natural and respectable station of a maritime power."[15]

In the course of narrating that same incident, Gibbon had the opportunity to note the role of changes in weather as distinguished from the constancy of climate in human affairs. Despite Britain's "natural and respectable station of a maritime power" already then, the British had to learn that "a superiority of naval strength will not always protect their country from a foreign invasion," as the Romans were assisted by the weather, which "proved favourable to their enterprise," and "under the cover of a thick fog, they escaped."[16] A few chapters earlier he had described how "a favourable wind" had helped the Gothic fleet to attain its goal in the Bosporus.[17] More striking than these references to sudden and apparently capricious shifts of weather, however, is his repeated polemic against any attempt to see such shifts as other than capricious, as in the resort of both pagans and Christians to what we would now call the pathetic fallacy. "Our habits of thinking," he commented, "so fondly [i.e., foolishly] connect the order of the universe with the fate of man, that this gloomy period of history has been decorated with inundations, earthquakes, uncommon meteors, praeternatural darkness, and a crowd of prodigies fictitious or exaggerated."[18] By far the most ambitious catalogue of such events appears at the end of chapter 43, where Gibbon enumerates in considerable scientific and clinical detail "the comets, the earthquake, and the plague, which astonished or afflicted the age of Justinian"—primarily, so it would seem, to deride a "superstition [that] involves the present danger with invisible terrors," by which "an affrighted people is more forcibly moved to expect the end of the world or to deprecate with servile homage the wrath of an avenging Deity."[19]

In describing the "misfortunes" brought about by such natural happenings in the Roman world—what British and American legal parlance, but probably not Gibbon, would still call "acts of God," namely, "action of uncontrollable natural forces in causing an accident, as the burning of a ship by lightning"[20]—Gibbon had his eye primarily on the drama of the human actors and on "the disgustful narration of [their] crimes and follies."[21] That eye, while sensitive to both folly and crime, was perhaps hypersensitive to folly. Sometimes the hypersensitivity seemed to lead to self-indulgence, as Gibbon found historical gossip about one or another particular human foible too delicious to resist. It was perhaps an awareness of such a tendency to self-indulgence that underlay his methodological declaration (as much, one is bound to suspect, to restrain the author's own preoccupations as to deflect the reader's curiosity): "The personal characters of the emperors, their victories, laws, follies and fortunes, can interest us no further than as they are connected with the general history of the Decline and Fall of the monarchy."[22] With occasional lapses from that methodology, a large number of them "in the obscurity of a learned language," Gibbon did concentrate on the public rather than the private import of follies and of crimes.

One special category of "follies" were those connected with religious faith and superstition (and it is, certainly by the author's own intention, not always clear whether or not Gibbon makes a distinction between "faith" and "superstition"). "Fear," Gibbon observed, "is commonly superstitious"; it was, in fact, "the parent of superstition," which was, in turn, "the parent of despotism."[23] In his descriptions, moreover, superstition was a thoroughly ecumenical phenomenon that "might be traced from Japan to Mexico":[24] the Egyptians of Alexandria were marked by "superstition and obstinacy";[25] the pagan Germans were "naked and unarmed to the blind terrors of superstition";[26] the Roman "multitude," by contrast with "the reflecting few," allowed spectacles to "inspire [their] superstitious mind with deep and solemn reverence";[27]

"zeal" (which is, for Gibbon, very similar to superstition) "has always formed the characteristic of the nation" of Israel;[28] the Christian Armenians were "a superstitious people";[29] perhaps above all, it was the Byzantine Christians who were afflicted by "the terrors of superstition," as their devotion to the icons made abundantly clear;[30] even the Neoplatonic philosophers, by contrast with "the ancient sages [who] had derided the popular superstition," "converted the study of philosophy into that of magic."[31] Among philosophers Zoroaster comes out considerably better, having manifested "a liberal concern for private and public happiness, seldom to be found among the groveling or visionary schemes of superstition."[32]

As for Christianity itself—whatever may have been the genuine intention of its founder, to whose own life and teachings Gibbon devotes only one paragraph of the *Decline and Fall,* and that not until the forty-seventh chapter[33]—Gibbon handled its relation to superstition in the same gingerly fashion with which he spoke about miracles. Speaking of the transition from paganism to Christianity, he noted that "the practice of superstition is so congenial to the multitude that . . . the fall of any system of mythology will most probably be succeeded by the introduction of some other mode of superstition." And although he went on to say that "the wisdom of Providence . . . interposed a genuine revelation" instead of this other mode of superstition, it should not escape the notice of sensitive readers that the three qualities that Gibbon enumerates as having characterized the superstitious folly of the Roman multitude— "their love of the marvellous and supernatural, their curiosity with regard to future events, and their strong propensity to extend their hopes and fears beyond the limits of the visible world"—find their precise counterparts in three of the elements of the Christian message to which he had just given credit for achieving its success: miracles, prophecy, and immortality.[34] It was only in his own time that the tyranny of superstition had been broken: "in almost every age except the present, [astrology] has maintained its dominion over the mind of man," which had now finally learned to "reject with contempt the arguments of superstition."[35]

By contrast with the way he condescended toward the vulgar and ignorant masses in his analysis of the follies of superstition, Gibbon treated sexual foibles as "the most amiable weaknesses of human nature," setting himself apart in his willingness "to find, or even to seek, in the revolutions of the world some traces of the mild and tender sentiments of domestic life" from "the unfeeling critics, who consider every amorous weakness as an indelible stain."[36] The emperor Marcus Aurelius—who is, if anyone is, the moral hero of the whole book, with his "severe" and "laborious" virtue, "the well-earned harvest of many a learned conference, of many a patient lecture, and many a midnight lucubration"[37]—had, according to Gibbon, "only [one] defective part of his character," a "mildness" that "dissembled . . . follies,"[38] including the profligacy of his son Commodus and the infidelity of his wife Faustina. While not condoning her conduct, Gibbon described it as having, "according to the prejudices of every age, reflected some disgrace on the injured husband." Gibbon did follow Tacitus's "honest pleasure in the contrast of barbarian [German] virtue with the dissolute conduct of the Roman ladies," noting that the "most dangerous enemy [of chastity] is the softness of the mind";[39] and he did manage in some measure to transcend the double standard in his disapproval of sexual excesses by men as well as by women.

His most explicit disapproval of such excesses is, however, reserved for what he repeatedly describes as "effeminacy," which is sometimes, though by no means always, his code word for male homosexuality. "Of the first fifteen emperors," he remarks, "Claudius was the only one whose taste in love was entirely correct," that is, exclusively heterosexual.[40] The follies of a prince who had "a soft and effeminate temper," whose "lust confounded the eternal distinctions of sex and species," or who indulged in "effeminate vices" and "the effeminate luxury of Oriental despotism"[41] were worse than immoral: they were dangerous to the public order. Gibbon appears to have associated such tendencies with the cultures of the Near East, speaking about "the effeminate troops of Egypt and Syria" and even about "contract[ing] a tincture of weakness and effeminacy from the soft climate of Syria."[42] Once again, however, it was what he understood to be the threat to public order and to military "valour" that made these "follies" a constituent part of his narrative; reviewing Christian legislation, "in defiance of every principle of justice," against private homosexual conduct, he attacked the "cruelty" of a persecution by which "our natural horror of vice may be abused as an engine of tyranny."[43]

If superstition was the special folly of ordinary people, often manipulated by tyrants in state and church, flaws of character were often the folly of the latter, "those tyrants whose capricious folly violated every law of nature and decency."[44] A unique example that "surpasses that of any other age or country" was provided by "the vices and follies of Elagabalus," or Heliogabalus (218–222), which one of the most steamy descriptive paragraphs of Gibbon's history recounts in prurient detail. In keeping with his resolve to concentrate on the public significance even of private follies, Gibbon went on to emphasize that while "the license of an eastern monarch is secluded from the eyes of curiosity by the inaccessible walls of the seraglio," this emperor "asserted without control his sovereign privilege of lust and luxury" and did so in "public scenes displayed before the Roman people,"[45] thus making his follies public and political events. Such flaws of character in an emperor were made worse when they were abetted by "all the various retinue of vice and folly."[46] Similarly, while the folly of young men in sowing their wild oats might seem relatively harmless or even amusing, it became dangerous to public life when the young men were "Caligula and Nero, Commodus and Caracalla, . . . all dissolute and inexperienced youths, educated in the purple, and corrupted by the pride of empire, the luxury of Rome, and the perfidious voice of flattery."[47] That pattern of folly, once established in the pagan Roman Empire, was perpetuated after it had declined, fallen, and been converted into the Christian Byzantine Empire, for, in Gibbon's formula, "Constantinople adopted the follies, though not the virtues, of ancient Rome."[48] Thus the Byzantine emperor Manuel Comnenus (who reigned from 1143 to 1180) was a valiant and intrepid warrior, but "no sooner did he return to Constantinople than he resigned himself to the arts and pleasures of a life of luxury."[49]

"But there is," Gibbon affirmed in his chapter on Alaric's sack of Rome, quoting Procopius, "a Providence that watches over innocence and folly," one to whose "peculiar care" he thought the emperor Honorius was especially entitled.[50] Although there had certainly been some *misfortunes* that helped to bring on the decline and fall of Rome and more than a few *follies,* Gibbon's investigation had also led to the uncovering of *crimes* as a contributing factor. Perhaps even more than misfortunes and follies, crimes belonged to the narrative "no further than as they are connected with the general history of the Decline and Fall of the monarchy." But directly upon defining that purpose Gibbon added: "Our constant attention to that great object will not suffer us to overlook a most important edict of Antoninus Caracalla, which communicated to all the free inhabitants of the empire the name and privileges of Roman citizens," an "unbounded liberality" that was in fact "the sordid result of avarice."[51] Gibbon's interest as the historian of the decline and fall of Rome was not in sins but in crimes, not in private transgressions but in public vices, for "whole generations may be swept away, by the madness of kings, in the space of a single hour."[52]

The distinction between public and private is important for the understanding of every question of ethics in its relation to *la raison d'état.* Invoking that very principle as he described the reign of the emperor Severus at the end of the second century, Gibbon early in his *History* defined with care and precision the part that moral considerations played and the part that they did not play in the affairs of state:

Falsehood and insincerity, unsuitable as they seem to the dignity of public transactions, offend us with a less degrading idea of meanness than when they are found in the intercourse of private life. In the latter, they discover a want of courage; in the other, only a defect of power; and, as it is impossible for the most able statesmen to subdue millions of followers and enemies by their own personal strength, the world, under the name of policy, seems to have granted them a very liberal indulgence of craft and dissimulation.

That did not constitute, for Gibbon, a carte blanche to lie and cheat, but only to do so if the needs of public life demanded. Therefore he continued:

Yet the arts of Severus cannot be justified by the most ample privileges of state-reason. He promised only to betray, he flattered only to ruin; and however he might occasionally bind himself by oaths and treaties, his conscience, obsequious to his interest, always released him from the inconvenient obligation.[53]

And "that," as Gibbon's younger French contemporary Antoine Boulay de la Meurthe is said to have remarked in 1804, "is worse than a crime, it is a blunder."

The capacity of distinguishing between public "crime" and private "sin" equipped the historian of the Roman Empire to handle the subtle relations between career and character in that remarkable sequence of "the unworthy successors of Augustus," whose "unparalleled vices, and the splendid theatre on which they were acted, have saved them from oblivion." They were, each with Gibbon's own Homeric epithet: "the dark unrelenting Tiberius, the furious Caligula, the stupid Claudius, the profligate and cruel Nero, the beastly Vitellius, and the timid inhuman Domitian." What made the "degeneracy" of such "monsters" the stuff not only of Roman gossip but of a *History of the Decline and Fall of the Roman Empire,* however, was that it "exterminated the ancient families of the republic, and was fatal to almost every virtue and every talent that arose in that unhappy period."[54] By contrast with the best years of the empire, when "it had hitherto been the peculiar felicity of the Romans, and in the worst of times their consolation, that the virtue of the emperors was active, and their vice indolent," these "monsters" and their yet more monstrous successors exhibited their vices in public and in such a way as to undercut the common weal: "Caracalla was the common enemy of mankind."[55] How their crimes made the pagan empire all too vulnerable to the enticements of the church and the ruthlessness of its imperial patrons became patent at the beginning of the fourth century when, in the power vacuum created by the abdication of the emperor Diocletian, the "vices and incapacity [of Maxentius, son of Diocletian's colleague Maximian] procured him the same exclusion from the dignity of Caesar which Constantine had deserved by a dangerous superiority of merit,"[56] a contrast that eventually led to Constantine's victory over Maxentius in the Battle of the Milvian Bridge, which Constantine's biographer Eusebius celebrated as the founding of the Christian empire.

At least one other crime deserves special mention: the "mean vice" and "abomination" of slavery.[57] As part of his review of the Roman social order, entitled "Of the Union and Internal Prosperity of the Roman Empire, in the Age of the Antonines," Gibbon took up the "unhappy condition of men who endured the weight, without sharing the benefits, of society."[58] When he noted in the course of that review, on the basis of Seneca, that "it was once proposed to discriminate the slaves by a peculiar habit, but it was justly apprehended that there might be some danger in acquainting them with their own numbers," he was preparing his readers for later chapters of the *History,* particularly the dramatic moment when, as Alaric, conqueror of Rome but emancipator of the slaves, was marching on the city, "the Gothic standard became the refuge of forty thousand Barbarian slaves, who had broke their chains, and aspired, under the command of their great deliverer, to revenge the injuries and the disgrace of their cruel servitude."[59] His description of the revolt of about eighty gladiators under the emperor Probus in 281, which ended with their defeat but also with "at least an honourable death, and the satisfaction of a just revenge,"[60] cannot fail to remind readers of the far more formidable insurrection led by Spartacus in 73 B.C.E., which Gibbon omitted presumably because it took place before the *terminus a quo* of his account. But it is clear from his language here about "the desperate courage" of the gladiators and "the inhuman sports of the amphitheatre" as well as from his comments in later chapters both about the "dangerous" and "bloody" "combats of the amphitheatre" and about "the custom of enslaving prisoners of war" during the Middle Ages,[61] that he saw in the gladiators and slaves not only the involuntary victims of a morally repugnant institution or even of the "inhuman and absurd cruelty" to which he referred in another context, but a body of "internal enemies, whose desperate insurrections had more than once reduced the republic to the brink of destruction" and might do so again in the empire.[62]

This "register of the crimes, follies, and misfortunes of mankind" was for Gibbon a more plausible and more instructive lesson of the history of the decline and fall of Rome than the apocalyptic belief that "considered every disaster that happened to the empire as an infallible symptom of an expiring world." Yet as a part of the causal nexus by which he sought to account for the decline and fall, it was, as Gibbon the philosopher would have liked to say, a "necessary" but not a "sufficient" condition, for the decline of Rome was, even more significantly, "the natural and inevitable effect of immoderate greatness."

Part Three

THE FATE OF EMPIRE

Instead of inquiring why the Roman empire was destroyed, we should rather be surprised that it had subsisted so long.

CHAPTER 6

The Founding of the
Christian Empire

The revival of Christian apocalypticism, albeit in a chastened form, may have been the most dramatic expression of the social triumph of the ancient church in its reaction to Alaric's sack of Rome in 410 C.E., but it was not, even in the Latin West, the only reaction to the decline and fall of Rome. To the Venerable Bede, for example, the fall does not seem to have been very important; it rated no more than a brief comment in his *History of the English Church and People* and that only with attention to the end of the Roman rule in Britain at the same time that "Rome fell to the Goths in the 1164th year after its foundation."[1] This may have been because he was writing three centuries or so afterwards or, more likely, because he was concentrating on the history of England. Nevertheless, it is to Bede that we owe the "sublime proverbial expression" quoted earlier: "As long as the Coliseum stands, Rome shall stand; when the Coliseum falls, Rome will fall; when Rome falls, the world will fall." After three hundred years the Coliseum still stood, though it was in ruins; Rome had fallen, several times in fact; and somehow the world too was still standing, although Bede was of course sure that he was living in the final age of world history. But in his *History* he did not make the sort of connection that Jerome and other Latin church fathers had made between the end of the Roman Empire in the West and the end of the world.

Other historians too, specifically three Eastern historians during the first half of the fifth century, dealt with the matter of that connection in a manner that, by contrast with Jerome's apocalypticism, must seem almost dispassionate, perhaps even callous. The first was Socrates Scholasticus in Constantinople, whom Gibbon cited in his narrative of the Arian controversy and whose "temperate and impartial freedom, very offensive to [Chrysostom's] blind admirers" he commended in his own account of the person and career of John Chrysostom.[2] A younger contemporary of Socrates, also in Constantinople, was Salmaninius Hermias Sozomenus (usually called Sozomen in English), in Gibbon's phrase "an original, though not impartial, witness" to some of the events he described, so that Gibbon was prepared to "admit [his] evidence" for some of them; as Gibbon noted, Sozomen "in general bear[s] . . . a resemblance" to Socrates, albeit with certain "remarkable difference[s]," including in some ways "a more liberal temper."[3] The third historian was Theodoret, in Antioch and Cyrrhus, whom Gibbon identified as "a bishop animated with apostolic fervour" (not a compliment in Gibbon's historical vocabulary), but whose "benevolent epistles" he used as a source in describing the "crowd of exiles, of fugitives, and of ingenuous captives" fleeing from North Africa before the invading Vandals in 439;[4] it was to Theodoret's condemnation for heresy in the fifth century and his posthumous restoration to good standing in the sixth that Gibbon devoted one of the most deliciously partisan of his many eloquent attacks on theological partisanship:

If these bishops [Theodoret and Ibas of Edessa], whether innocent or guilty, were annihilated in the sleep of death, they would not probably be awakened by the clamour which, after an hundred years, was raised over their grave. If they were already in the fangs of the daemon, their torments could neither be aggravated nor assuaged by human industry. If in the company of saints and angels they enjoyed the rewards of piety, they must have smiled at the idle fury of the theological insects who still crawled on the surface of the earth. The foremost of these insects, the emperor of the Romans [Justinian], darted his sting, and distilled his venom.[5]

All three of these Eastern historians were contemporary to the historical drama of 410 and following.[6]

Socrates devoted only one paragraph of his *History* to the events of 410. "About this same time [that is, when Porphyry was bishop of Antioch and Innocent I bishop of Rome]," it begins, "it came about that Rome was captured by the barbarians." "A certain Alaric," the narrative continues, "a barbarian who had been an ally of the Romans [that is to say, of course, of the Romans whose capital was Constantinople], and had served as an ally with the emperor Theodosius in the war against the usurper Eugenius, having on that account been honored with Roman [i.e., Constantinopolitan] dignities, found his good fortune too much to bear." "Withdrawing from Constantinople," therefore, Alaric "went into the Western territories" of Constantinople's empire. The climax of his campaign came when "the barbarians that were with him, destroying everything in their path, at last took Rome itself." Having captured Rome, "they pillaged it, burning a very great number of the magnificent structures and other admirable works of art that it contained."[7] And then, "in mockery of the dignity of the emperor [in Constantinople], Alaric proclaimed a certain Attalus emperor," as Gibbon explains, "on the throne of the unworthy Honorius."[8]

The account of Sozomen is similar, though not identical. "Alaric, the leader of the Goths," Sozomen wrote, "advanced to Rome and laid siege to it." Eventually, "after the siege had lasted some time, there had been fearful ravages in the city because of famine and pestilence." Therefore "many of the slaves, as well as most of those within the walls who were barbarians by race, deserted to Alaric's side." The final capture of the city, however, was by "treachery" rather than sheer force. Alaric "permitted each of his followers to seize as much of the wealth of the Romans as he was able, and to plunder all the houses."[9] There was, however, one highly significant exception, by which, in Gibbon's words, "Alaric, when he forced his entrance into a vanquished city, discovered . . . some regard for the laws of humanity and religion."[10] As Sozomen reports, "from respect toward the apostle Peter, [Alaric] commanded that the large and very spacious church erected around his tomb should be an asylum." (This was what archeologists now usually call "Old Saint Peter's," the basilica begun by the emperor Constantine in about 324 and finished by his son, the emperor Constantius, about thirty years later.) The declaration that Saint Peter's was out of bounds was, Sozomen adds, "the only cause which prevented the entire demolition of Rome,"[11] although, as Gibbon reminded his readers, "the holy precincts of the Vatican and the apostolic churches could receive [only] a very small proportion of the Roman people."[12]

In their accounts, both Socrates and Sozomen tell the story of a monk whom Alaric met on his way to Rome. The monk admonished him not to sack Rome and not to take pleasure in bloodshed, but Alaric replied with the highly portentous words: "I am not going on this course of my own will; but there is a something that irresistibly impels me daily, saying 'Proceed to Rome, and desolate that city!' " Whatever the relation between the two historical accounts may be, Walter Kaegi is certainly correct when he observes, in commenting on the anecdote of the monk who met Alaric on the way to Rome: "Socrates obviously regards the event as important and a manifest demonstration of the vanity of worldly power."[13] Both Socrates and Sozomen took the whole story of Alaric's sack of Rome as a cautionary tale that taught the appropriate moral lesson. "All persons of good sense," Sozomen wrote, "were aware that the calamities which this siege brought upon the Romans [meaning here the inhabitants of the city of Old Rome, although, as noted earlier, the word 'Romans' came sometimes to mean 'Byzantines'] were indications of divine wrath sent to chastise them for their luxury, their debauchery, and their manifold acts of injustice toward each other, as well as toward strangers."[14]

As they stand, these words seem to be little more than a parallel to the attacks on pagan Roman immorality that are found also in Western Christian writers from Tertullian to Augustine and Orosius and beyond. But in the last book of Sozomen's *Ecclesiastical History,* such moralizing is sounded in counterpoint with another and more central theme. Having described the invasions of Italy by the Huns and then by "Uldis, the leader of the barbarous tribes who dwell near the Ister," Sozomen immediately went on to point up a striking contrast: "When affairs were so helpless" at Old Rome in the West, he wrote, "God gave manifest proofs of special favor toward the present reign" of the Christian emperor Theodosius the Younger in New Rome, Constantinople.[15] And then to underscore the contrast still more sharply, he continued: "Thus was the Eastern empire preserved from the evils of war and governed with high order. This ran contrary to all expectations, for its ruler was still a young man. In the meantime, the Western empire fell a prey to disorders, because many tyrants arose [there]."[16] The defeat of enemies foreign and domestic by the royal house of Theodosius was to Sozomen a clear manifestation of divine mercy, indeed a victory by God himself, "for He increases the emperor in years and in government, and every conspiracy and war concocted against him has been overthrown of itself."[17] In documenting this thesis in Book Nine of his *Ecclesiastical History,* Sozomen was carrying out the purpose announced in his dedicatory epistle to Emperor Theodosius the

Younger to devote that book of his *History* to "your Christ-loving and most innocent Majesty, which may God always preserve in unbroken good will, triumphing greatly over [your] enemies, having all things under your feet, and transmitting the holy empire to your sons' sons with the approbation of Christ."[18]

Not surprisingly, Sozomen in that dedicatory epistle also called upon biblical typology (as well as upon classical Greek philosophy) for his description of the "Christ-loving and innocent" emperor Theodosius. Characterizing him as a philosopher-king who spent his days on government and his nights on scholarship, Sozomen likened Theodosius to King Solomon, "the wisest son of David." But he quickly added that Theodosius excelled Solomon in virtue, for Solomon had been corrupted by becoming a slave to his pleasures, while Theodosius had proved himself to be "an autocrat not only over men, but also over the passions of soul and body."[19] This is, to be sure, not a very subtle use of biblical typology for a panegyric to a king—not so subtle, for example, as was to be the application to Theodosius's successor, Justinian, of the biblical title "Melchizedek," because he was king and priest in one. Socrates Scholasticus too employed a biblical prototype in his praise of Theodosius, but one that went far beyond the cliché of calling him "Solomon." After anticipating the use of Melchizedek as a type for Justinian by asserting that the emperor Theodosius had in his meekness gone beyond all those who had ever been priests, he continued:

What is recorded of Moses in the Book of Numbers [12:3], "Now the man Moses was very meek, more than all men that were on the face of the earth," may most justly be applied in the present. For the emperor Theodosius is "more meek than all men that are upon the face of the earth." It is because of this meekness that God has subdued his enemies without military conflict.

Locating Theodosius in the succession of biblical heroes and saints, Socrates added: "For the God of the universe has granted to this most devout emperor in our times aid of a similar kind to what was vouchsafed to the righteous in the past."[20]

It is instructive to attend closely to the biblical exegesis at work in this portrait of Theodosius. Socrates applied to the emperor the word "meek," the same Greek word that is used by Jesus in the Beatitudes of the Sermon on the Mount: "Blessed are the meek, for they shall inherit the earth" (Matt. 5:5). This Beatitude, like the others, had received its classic exposition among the Greek Christian theologians of the fourth century at the hands of Gregory of Nyssa. Explaining such meekness as "a standard of virtue [that is] attainable in the life of the flesh," Gregory described the reward, "they shall inherit the earth," as that "supercelestial earth which is reserved to be the inheritance of those who have led a life of virtue," just as the "kingdom" in the preceding Beatitude was grossly misunderstood if one took it "to indicate such things as earthly kingship entails" among "those who would emphasize the importance of power."[21] John Chrysostom—whom Theodoret called "the great teacher of the world"[22] and whose oratorical "compositions," in Gibbon's words, "have been compared with the most splendid models of Attic, or at least of Asiatic, eloquence," so that the "multitudes" of Constantinople "preferred the eloquent and edifying discourses of their archbishop to the amusements of the theatre or the circus"[23]—had been a bit less otherworldly in his own exegesis of the Sermon on the Mount. "For neither in speaking of any spiritual thing," he explained in his comment on this Beatitude, "does he exclude such as are in the present life; nor again in promising such as are in our life, does he limit his promise to that kind."[24] From these words the conclusion would seem to be necessary that for Chrysostom "the passage must mean that Christ sought to motivate his hearers both by the prospect of eternal glory and by the promise of temporal gain, a literal 'earth' that they would possess by inheritance if they practiced true meekness."[25] But Socrates takes that kind of this-worldly exegesis a giant step further when he applies this Beatitude specifically to the emperor Theodosius, for when the emperor was "meek," he inherited the earth with a political literalness that filled his admirers with wonder and his enemies with dread.

Even more significant in this typological exegesis of Socrates is his identification of Theodosius, the "most devout" Christian emperor, with Moses. In this identification, as in his *History* as a whole, Socrates was patterning himself after his predecessor and the founder of ecclesiastical history among the Greeks, Eusebius of Caesarea; similarly, Theodoret explicitly declared his intention to "begin my history from the period at which [Eusebius's] terminates."[26] As the leading Eusebius scholar of the twentieth century, Edward Schwartz, once observed, "in Greek historiography it is almost a law that a work of history that has made some impact is continued in a sequel, and that happened also to the *Ecclesiastical History* of Eusebius."[27] It happened also, although Schwartz does not mention this, to another work by Eusebius, his *Life of Constantine*, of which Socrates says: "Eusebius Pamphilius has in magnificent terms recorded the praises of the emperor" Constantine,[28] for in this as in almost everything else, Eusebius, in Gibbon's phrase, "studied and gratified the taste of his master."[29] When Eusebius took up the task of narrating what he called the "miracles more wonderful than fables"[30] of which he had been an eyewitness and to some extent even a participant, he worked out a full-scale typology based on the life of Moses with which to describe the emperor Constantine. Moses, the future deliverer of his people, had been reared "in the very palaces and bosoms of the oppressors," Eusebius writes, for Moses at the court of Pharaoh was "instructed in all the wisdom they possessed" (Acts 7:22). In the same way Constantine "dwelt, as that other servant of God had done, in the very home of the tyrants," that is, in the court of Diocletian and of Galerius. But eventually the time came for Moses to "estrange himself in word and deed from the tyrants by whom he had been brought up"; so also Constantine, "who was shortly to become their destroyer," came out from among "the tyrants of our day," who had dared to wage war against God himself by persecuting his church.

When the appointed time came for Constantine to emerge as the liberator, he, like Moses, prevailed over those with whom he had been reared. Speaking in 315 or so at the dedication of a church in Tyre, Eusebius exulted that "now we no longer perceive the lofty arm and the celestial right hand of our all-gracious God and universal King by hearsay merely or report, but observe so to speak in very deed and with our own eyes that the declarations recorded long ago are faithful and true."[31] Just a few years earlier the same "lofty arm and celestial right hand" manifested in the victory of Moses over the hosts of Pharaoh at the Red Sea had been manifested again in the victory of Constantine over Maxentius at the Milvian Bridge on 27 October 312. As he pondered these events, Eusebius, according to Schwartz, added Book Nine to his *Ecclesiastical History* in 315. In the dramaturgy of that book, the victory of Constantine became a grand reenactment of the scene recorded in the fifteenth chapter of the Book of Exodus. "Those who obtained the victory from God," Eusebius writes, "if not in words, at least in deeds, like Moses the great servant of God, and those who were with him, fittingly sang as they had sung against the impious tyrant of old, saying, 'Let us sing unto the Lord, for he hath gloriously glorified himself, horse and rider hath he cast into the sea.' "[32] What Judah Goldin says about the original song that Miriam the sister of Moses had danced and sung with the daughters of Israel applies to this as well:

The Song at the Sea is serious in the extreme, and there is no mistaking what this ode proclaims: the triumph is God's triumph, from beginning to end. He is the truly exalted, and to Him even horses and chariots and top-flight officers are as nothing![33]

According to Eusebius, the events of that ancient victory had now been reenacted in this great victory:

As in the time of Moses himself and of the ancient God-beloved race of the Hebrews, "he cast Pharaoh's chariots and host into the sea . . . ," in the same way Maxentius also with his soldiers and bodyguards "went down into the depths like a stone," when he fled before the power of God which was with Constantine.[34]

Thus Constantine and his hosts celebrated the victory that God had now granted also to them over the tyrant.

And so they entered into the Promised Land. The conclusion seems incontrovertible that the decisive event in the history of Rome was, in the interpretation of Eusebius in the fourth century and of the fifth-century historians who continued his narrative, not what happened when Alaric or Attila marched to the gates of Old Rome (about which Socrates and Sozomen said so little and Theodoret said nothing), but what happened when Constantine marched to Old Rome and then when he marched on to New Rome; in Gibbon's words, "the foundation of Constantinople, and the establishment of the Christian religion, were the immediate and memorable consequences of this revolution."[35] For this historical interpretation, it was essential to hold to the legitimacy of Constantine's claim to the imperial throne, for which God himself had destined him. To commemorate the victory, Constantine had a statue of himself erected and commanded that the following inscription should stand on the statue: "By this savior sign, the true test of bravery, I saved and freed your city from the yoke of the tyrant, and restored the senate and the Roman people, freed, to their ancient fame and splendor."[36] And Eusebius himself, who is our only source for this text of Constantine's inscription, tells us in the following book of his *Ecclesiastical History* that "Constantine the most mighty victor . . . reconquered the East . . . and formed the Roman Empire as in the days of old into a single unified whole."[37] To Socrates and Sozomen it was equally essential that Theodosius, too, be acknowledged as the legitimate Caesar.

The theme of all these historians, therefore, was "continuity" or "succession." That is the word with which Eusebius began his *Ecclesiastical History*, "the successions from the holy apostles";[38] and at the end of Book Seven he reviewed the work up to that point: "Having concluded the subject of the successions, from the birth of our Savior to the destruction of the places of prayer" under Diocletian.[39] The concept of "succession" or "continuity" became the leitmotiv of the entire work.[40] Even Jacob Burckhardt, who characterized Eusebius as "the first thoroughly dishonest historian of antiquity," went on to affirm the centrality of this principle of continuity in the Later Roman Empire, which "was never in doubt, even for a moment," despite dynastic wars and usurpations, even in the darkest days of Byzantine intrigue and tyranny.[41] As documentation of that continuity, Eusebius made the succession of the Roman emperors what one eminent historian has called "the backbone of the chronology in the *History*."[42] Yet it is important to note, as other scholars have pointed out, that "there is a lower and scarcely less important unit [of chronology]—the period of the episcopate of an eminent bishop, usually a bishop of Rome."[43]

In Constantinople that continuity took the form of the name "the New Rome." Socrates speaks of it this way in the first book of his *History:* "The city named after him, which had previously been called Byzantium, he enlarged, surrounded with massive walls, and adorned with various edifices," above all, of course, with the Church of the Holy Wisdom, the first version of what was to become under his successor Justinian the Christian answer to the temple of Solomon, Hagia Sophia. "Having rendered it equal to imperial Rome," Socrates goes on, "he named it Constantinople, establishing by law that it should be designated New Rome. This law was engraved on a pillar of stone erected in public view in the Strategium, near the Emperor's equestrian statue."[44] That affirmation of continuity as "New Rome" served as the basis for Canon III promulgated by the second of the ecumenical councils of the church, held at Constantinople in 381: "The bishop of Constantinople shall have the prerogative of honor [directly] after the bishop of Rome, because Constantinople is New Rome." That canon of 381 was reaffirmed and elaborated in the so-called twenty-eighth canon of the Council of Chalcedon in 451:

We also do enact and decree the same things concerning the privileges of the most holy Church of Constantinople, which is New Rome. For the Fathers rightly granted privileges to the [ecclesiastical] throne of Old Rome, because it was the imperial city. And the 150 most religious bishops [at the council of 381], actuated by the same consideration, gave equal privileges to the most holy throne of New Rome, justly judging that the city which is honored with the sovereignty and the Senate, and enjoys equal privileges with the old imperial Rome, should, in ecclesiastical matters, also be magnified as she is, and rank after her.[45]

This was to have far-reaching consequences in the jurisdictional and even the doctrinal history of the church from the middle of the fifth century to the present.[46]

In the present context, however, such declarations are important for the understanding that Constantinople had of itself in relation to what Gibbon called "the decline and fall of the Roman Empire," for as New Rome, it was "the city which is honored with the sovereignty and the Senate, and enjoys equal privileges with the old imperial Rome"; and the basic argument of both decrees, in 381 and again in 451, was that the civic and legal standing of New Rome should also serve to define its ecclesiastical and canonical authority. The continuity of "old imperial Rome" lay now with "New Rome," the city of the most holy and God-fearing emperors. It should be remembered that in 381, when that claim was put forward, the imperial throne in Constantinople was occupied by Emperor Theodosius the Great, whose decree of 392 establishing the church as the official religion of the empire was, in the words of Shirley Jackson Case, "the Magna Carta of orthodox Christianity's supremacy over all competitors in the religious arena."[47] He was the grandfather and namesake of the Theodosius to whom Sozomen dedicated his *History* and of whose accomplishments Socrates spoke with such unstinted admiration. According to Sozomen, Constantine had, by the intervention of God in the form of a vision by night and "in obedience to the words of God," chosen the old city of Byzantium as the location of the new capital to bear his name. It was to be a fresh new beginning "not polluted by altars, Grecian temples, nor sacrifices,"[48] but at the same time it was to stand as the capital of the Roman Empire in unbroken succession with the ancient days of the Caesars. It was, the fifth-century historians were sure, providential that he should have done so when and where he did, for by that act the continuity of the empire was preserved just in the nick of time. Or, in Gibbon's language, "as some decent mixture of prodigy and fable has, in every age, been supposed to reflect a becoming majesty on the origin of great cities, the emperor was desirous of ascribing his resolution, not so much to the uncertain counsels of human policy, as to the infallible and eternal decrees of divine wisdom."[49]

What fell to Alaric's marauding Goths in 410, consequently, was "Old Rome," not "New Rome," and certainly not the Roman Empire, which had been assured of its continuity through divine providence by the transfer of its capital from Italy to the Bosporus. For the Byzantines, too, there were therefore "two cities"; but these were not, as they were for Jerome and for the Westerners who followed his lead, old pagan Rome and new Christian Rome, both in the same geographical location. Rather they were "Old Rome," which retained its primacy of honor in the church at least as long as it remained orthodox in its doctrine and respected its sister churches, and "New Rome," which had taken over Old Rome's place of honor in the empire and which eventually claimed on those grounds to have acquired also a commensurate standing in the church. The privileged status of New Rome as the city of God's own choosing became a persistent theme of Byzantine polemics against the Latins for a thousand years. The great trauma for the East, therefore, was not the decline and fall of Old Rome in the fifth century, but the fall of New Rome a whole millennium later, in 1453. Contemporary accounts of the atrocities of the invaders but also of the naive confidence that the city could never fall do carry many echoes of the apocalyptic language of Jerome. But it should not be forgotten that the catastrophe of 1453 had been foreshadowed by the tragedy of the Fourth Crusade in 1204, of which Sir Steven Runciman says: "There never was a greater crime against humanity than the Fourth Crusade,"[50] when New Rome was pillaged not by Goths or Huns or Turks, but by the thieves and murderers who had come from Old Rome in the West to rescue the Holy Places in Palestine. But until that calamity, the city of Constantinople—which, in the words of Edward Gibbon, "appears to have been formed by Nature for the centre and capital of a great monarchy . . . [with] the prospect of beauty, of safety, and of wealth"[51]— had stood, even for the Latin West,[52] as the embodiment of the ideal of the Christian empire and of the continuity of Rome despite the events associated with what is usually identified as its "decline and fall."

CHAPTER 7

The Inevitable Effect of Immoderate Greatness

As the very title of his work indicates, Gibbon did not regard the events he was recounting as a beginning but as an end. For the Byzantine historians of the fourth and fifth centuries, the founding of the Christian empire by Constantine may have been the leitmotiv of their commentaries on the history of their own times, but for Gibbon the same history was a history of the decline and fall of the Roman Empire. That was, moreover, the very reason he selected it as the topic for his book, as he acknowledged in one of his most revelatory paragraphs:

The rise of a city, which swelled into an empire, may deserve, as a singular prodigy, the reflection of a philosophic mind. But the decline of Rome was the natural and inevitable effect of immoderate greatness. Prosperity ripened the principle of decay; the causes of destruction multiplied with the extent of conquest; and, as soon as time or accident had removed the artificial supports, the stupendous fabric yielded to the pressure of its own weight. The story of its ruin is simple and obvious; and, instead of inquiring why the Roman empire was destroyed, we should rather be surprised that it had subsisted so long.[1]

More perhaps than any other single statement in the *Decline and Fall,* [2] that represents the official verdict of the coroner; yet it is only part of an ongoing autopsy that is always complex and frequently ambiguous. Although "the vain and transitory scenes of human greatness are unworthy of a serious thought"[3] and "a just but melancholy reflection embitter[s] . . . the noblest of human enjoyments,"[4] not only the rise but also the decline and fall of a civilization could "deserve the reflection of a philosophic mind."

Behind the decline and fall of the Roman Empire—behind it chronologically as well as logically—lay the decline and fall of the Roman Republic. "Although I have devoted myself to write the annals of a declining monarchy," Gibbon declared in his chapter on Roman jurisprudence, "I shall embrace the occasion to breathe the pure and invigorating air of the republic."[5] Originally, "it had been the object of Augustus to conceal the introduction of monarchy."[6] But after Augustus "the fine theory of a republic insensibly vanished, and made way for the more natural and substantial feelings of monarchy," in which "the Romans, after the fall of the republic, combated only for the choice of masters."[7] In its finest hour, the age of the Antonines, the empire showed the marks of its republican origins, for "such princes deserved the honour of restoring the republic, had the Romans of their days been capable of enjoying a rational freedom."[8] From time to time such intimations of the greatness of the republic continued to manifest themselves whenever "the image of the republic was revived, after a long interval," only to end each time in proof of "the decline of the Roman state, far different from its infancy."[9] The forms of the Roman republic survived the reality for centuries, because they "still lived in the minds of the people."[10] But eventually, though the authority of the senate might momentarily be "fortified by the actual weakness of a declining monarchy," even these "frail and mouldering" forms declined and fell, until in 552 "the fate of the senate suggests an awful lesson of the vicissitudes of human affairs," as "after a period of thirteen centuries, the institution of Romulus expired."[11] In the words of the emperor Julian, as translated (or paraphrased) by Gibbon, "the Roman republic . . . is now reduced to want and wretchedness."[12]

Of course the empire, too, had been reduced to want and wretchedness. If its fall was "the natural and inevitable effect of immoderate greatness," the internal causes of the decline and fall were to be sought in the greatness itself. It lay in Gibbon's interest as historian and dramatist, therefore, to take the full measure of that greatness. "The greatness of Rome," Gibbon quoted the Roman historian Ammianus Marcellinus as declaring, "was founded on the rare and almost incredible alliance of virtue and fortune."[13] It had, in many ways, found its embodiment in "the first and greatest of the Caesars," Julius, who had managed to combine "the commanding superiority of soul, the generous clemency, and the various genius, which could reconcile and unite the love of pleasure, the thirst of knowledge, and the fire of ambition."[14] Although ambition could be "daring" or "crafty" or "rash,"[15] it was also prerequisite to greatness, as Gibbon made clear in his trenchant portrait of Diocletian:

The valour of Diocletian was never found inadequate to his duty, or to the occasion; but he appears not to have possessed the daring and generous spirit of a hero, who courts danger and fame, disdains artifice, and boldly challenges the allegiance of his equals. His abilities were useful rather than splendid; a vigorous mind, improved by the study of mankind, dexterity and application in business; a judicious mixture of liberality and economy, of mildness and rigour; profound dissimulation under the disguise of military frankness; steadiness to pursue his ends; flexibility to vary his means; and above all the great art of submitting his own passions, as well as those of others, to the interest of his ambition, and of colouring his ambition with the most specious pretences of justice and public utility.[16]

The characteristic form that this "virtue" of ambition took in the history of Rome was what Gibbon usually describes as military "valour," whose ambiguity in his account is symbolized by the paradoxical juxtaposition, just two paragraphs apart, of two aphorisms: "Those who refuse the sword must renounce the sceptre" and "The fame of warriors is built on the destruction of human kind."[17]

Only an ignorant barbarian would suppose that "military virtue and success" were intrinsically incompatible with culture, scholarship, and science, for "the science of war . . . constituted the more rational force of Greece and Rome."[18] When it was combined, as it had been "in the ages of freedom and victory," with the "severe simplicity" of the Romans and with the "superiority" that came from "discipline and temper," such "virtue and military genius," even during the later days of the empire, could be decisive.[19] Indeed, it was "the discipline of the legions, which alone, after the extinction of every other virtue, had propped the greatness of the state."[20] So long as that discipline was maintained and the armies were commanded by leaders who had received a liberal education and were equally at home in civilian and military society, there could be a balance between the two parts of the paradox.[21] In its days of glory during the Punic wars, Rome had had a population of "intrepid courage," in which "every citizen was trained, from his earliest youth, in the discipline and exercises of a soldier" and every senator had seen military service.[22] Conversely, "emperor [*impera-*

tor]" had meant "general of the Roman armies" before it meant "sovereign of the Roman world": the emperors "appeared in the field at the head of their armies," but their "degenerate successors" did not.[23] Even at the end of the third century, when the Roman legions confronted a peasant rebellion in Gaul, their "strength of union and discipline obtained an easy victory."[24] But it was the lesson of these later centuries of the empire that "in times of confusion every active genius finds the place assigned him by nature," and that therefore "in a general state of war military merit is the road to glory and to greatness."[25]

Such military merit was irresistibly tempted to overreach itself and to become an "immoderate greatness" whose very success would be its own undoing, as a series of changes "corrupted military discipline and prepared the ruin of the empire."[26] Gibbon proposed it as a rule of thumb "calculated by the ablest politicians[,] that no state, without being soon exhausted, can maintain above the hundredth part of its members in arms and idleness."[27] There is scarcely a chapter of the *Decline and Fall,* especially in the early part of the book, without some reference to the processes of degeneration within the army. Thus in the very first chapter, his observations on the technology of armaments lead to the comment that "the use of them in the field gradually became more prevalent, in proportion as personal valour and military skill declined with the Roman empire."[28] Under Caracalla, "the vigour of the soldiers, instead of being confirmed by the severe discipline of camps, melted away in the luxury of cities," which led to "luxurious idleness" and to a "haughty laziness" that was "impatient of the restraints of discipline, and careless of the blessings of public tranquillity."[29] So it came about that "the military order had levelled in wild anarchy the power of the prince, the laws of the senate, and even the discipline of the camps."[30] Soon the attributes begin to shift, and we find Gibbon speaking about the "valour" of the barbarian Germans and contrasting it with the morale of the Roman armies, in which "the introduction of luxury had enervated the vigour, and a spirit of disobedience and sedition had relaxed the discipline."[31] They were in no condition and in no mood to defend the city.[32] Their "insolence" and their "precarious loyalty" and "licentiousness" had made them a threat to the state rather than its bulwark.[33] Increasingly, the Roman armies were made up of Germans, and even commanded by them; and so, "while the republic was guarded, or threatened, by the doubtful sword of the Barbarians, the last sparks of the military flame were finally extinguished in the minds of the Romans."[34]

A special case of "immoderate greatness" had been the growth in the power of the Praetorian guard, "whose licentious fury was the first symptom and cause of the decline of the Roman empire." Augustus, "sensible that laws might colour, but that arms alone could maintain, his usurped dominion, had gradually formed this powerful body of guards, in constant readiness to protect his person, to awe the senate, and either to prevent or to crush the first motions of rebellion." Although, Gibbon continued, "such formidable servants are always necessary, but often fatal, to the throne of despotism," the Praetorians quickly got out of hand:

By thus introducing the Praetorian guards, as it were, into the palace and senate, the emperors taught them to perceive their own strength, and the weakness of the civil government; to view the vices of their masters with familiar contempt, and to lay aside that reverential awe which distance only, and mystery, can preserve towards an imaginary power. In the luxurious idleness of an opulent city, their pride was nourished by the sense of their irresistible weight; nor was it possible to conceal from them that the person of the sovereign, the authority of the senate, the public treasure, and the seat of empire, were all in their hands.. To divert the Praetorian bands from these dangerous reflections the firmest and best established princes were obliged to mix blandishments with commands, rewards with punishments, to flatter their pride, indulge their pleasures, connive at their irregularities, and to purchase their precarious faith by a liberal donative.[35]

But "the last insult on the Roman name" and "the most insolent excess of military license" took place on 28 March 193, when the Praetorian guards auctioned off the empire to the highest bidder, "the wretched Julian," who on 2 June of the same year "was conducted into a private apartment of the baths of the palace, and beheaded as a common criminal, after having purchased, with an immense treasure, an anxious and precarious reign of only sixty-six days."[36] Once unleashed, however, such a military and political force was difficult to control. The emperor Severus strove to reform the Praetorian guard, but as it turned out the Praetorian prefect became an *éminence grise,* "not only at the head of the army, but of the finances, and even of the law."[37] A succession of emperors—Alexander, Maximus, Maxentius, and Maximian—strove to tame them, but in vain.³⁸ Under "the prudent measures of Diocletian, the numbers of the Praetorians were insensibly reduced, [and] their privileges abolished," but it was only after they had once more become guilty of insurrection that "those haughty troops . . . were for ever suppressed by Constantine."³⁹

The proclivity of military "valour" for such *hybris* and then for decadence was not a peculiarly Roman weakness, however; it was endemic to every army, perhaps to every society. After describing the "valour" of the barbarians in his earliest chapters, Gibbon went on to chart the course of this endemic disease as it spread also among Rome's conquerors. The Goths had "marched with the proud confidence that their invincible valour would decide the fate of the Roman empire."⁴⁰ But after it had done so, "the luxury of Italy had been less effectual to soften the temper than to relax the courage of the Goths; and they had imbibed the vices, without imitating the arts and institutions, of civilised society."⁴¹ The Vandals were the conquerors of Roman Africa, but "in three generations prosperity and a warm climate had dissolved the hardy virtue of the Vandals, who insensibly became the most luxurious of mankind."⁴² The Turks "mowed down their patient enemies like hemp or grass," but "the conquerors were enervated by luxury, which is always fatal except to an industrious people."⁴³ Earlier monarchs of the Armenians had been characterized by "manly virtues," but eventually this nation too "degenerated" into "timid indolence" and became "pusillanimous."⁴⁴ And the Christians, who had endured with "invincible valour" their persecution by Nero, Decius, and Diocletian, were destroyed instead by their success and they "contracted the insolent vices of prosperity."⁴⁵ Their "intolerant spirit, which disgraced the triumph of Christianity, contributed to the loss of the most important province of the West," the North Africa of Augustine.⁴⁶ And so when "the Roman troops . . . degenerated . . . from the valour of their ancestors,"⁴⁷ they were following what amounted to a universal law. But in their case, when "the enervated soldiers abandoned their own and the public defence," the outcome was that "their pusillanimous indolence may be considered as the immediate cause of the downfall of the empire."⁴⁸

It was not, however, the only cause. Although there are individual passages in which Gibbon does give that impression, he did recognize that the causes were far more complex. "An extensive empire," he wrote,

THE INEVITABLE EFFECT OF IMMODERATE GREATNESS / 85

must be supported by a refined system of policy and oppression: in the centre, an absolute power, prompt in action and rich in resources; a swift and easy communication with the extreme parts; fortifications to check the first effort of rebellion; a regular administration to protect and punish; and a well-disciplined army to inspire fear, without provoking discontent and despair.[49]

In such catalogues of political and military factors, his Marxist critics have identified as his major shortcoming an inadequate attention to the economic determination of history, and even his defenders have acknowledged that this factor sometimes seems to have been lost amid all the moralizing about "virtue" and "valour." Nevertheless, it is unfair to suppose that Gibbon completely ignored economic illnesses in his autopsy, for in economics no less than in politics and military morality the decline and fall of Rome was for him "the natural and inevitable consequence of immoderate greatness." Indeed, it is arguable that for Gibbon a fatal flaw of the Romans was that they themselves had ignored economic illnesses and economic realities, especially "the enormous disproportion of wealth,"[50] as they constructed and expanded their empire. Although it remained true long after Gibbon that, in Bury's words, "for the inquiry touching the revenue of the empire we have not sufficient data to make even an approximate estimate," Gibbon was "inclined to believe," on the basis of the bits and pieces of evidence surviving from the early economic history of the Roman Empire, that "so ample a revenue must have been fully adequate to all the expenses of the moderate government instituted by Augustus."[51] The problem was, once again, that this "moderate government" was soon infected by "immoderate greatness," for which such revenue was insufficient; "the victories of the republic added less to the wealth than to the power of Rome," while "the nobles of Rome were more tenacious of property than of freedom."[52] Yet even a "philosopher" would have to "confess," Gibbon opined, "that the desire of spoil is a more rational provocation than the vanity of conquest."[53] At the same time he believed that avarice was "the blindest of human passions,"[54] blinder even than "the vanity of conquest."

The mutual relations among these various causes underlay Gibbon's summary statement, at the point of transition in his history from the pagan to the Christian empire, that the events of the early fourth century had "contributed to the decline of the empire by the expense of blood and treasure, and by the perpetual increase, as well of the taxes as of the military establishment."[55] The "expense of treasure" was a recurring theme, signaled by his repeated use of the verb "exhaust." Already in the third century, "the industry of the people was discouraged and exhausted by a long series of oppression"; just before Alaric's invasion and sack of Rome early in the fifth century, the empire was in a "feeble and exhausted state"; efforts to protect Rome by subsidies to the barbarians served only "to exhaust what yet remained of the treasures of the republic"; later in the same century, as the Visigoths were invading, "the public confidence was lost; the resources of the state were exhausted"; and the Greeks of the Byzantine Empire whom the Arabs confronted had been "exhausted by the Persian war" and then "were exhausted by the calamities of war and the loss of their fairest provinces."[56] Efforts to cope with the economic woes of the empire frequently produced an opposite effect. Under the emperor Julian, for example, the empire experienced "the rapacious arts of monopoly," incisively summarized by Gibbon in a one-sentence definition: "In this unequal contest, in which the produce of the land is claimed by one party as his exclusive property; is used by another as a lucrative object of trade; and is required by a third for the daily and necessary support of life; all the profits of the intermediate agents are accumulated on the head of the defenceless consumers." But the emperor's attempt to counteract the monopolies by fixing prices only made things worse.[57]

Underlying this monopoly of grain was an inequitable distribution of the land itself, which was concentrated in "those ample estates, to which the ruin of Italy is originally imputed": even before the empire, "in the age which preceded the fall of the republic it was computed that only two thousand citizens were possessed of any independent substance" in real estate.[58] The identification of agriculture and the army as fundamental problems led to the ingenious expedient of putting the soldiers to work on the farms; "an army thus employed," Gibbon suggested, "constituted perhaps the most useful, as well as the bravest, portion of the Roman subjects."[59] It was, in any case, too little and too late, for "since the age of Tiberius, the decay of agriculture had been felt in Italy; and it was a subject of complaint that the life of the Roman people depended on the accidents of the winds and waves,"[60] because they had to import most of their food. For that reason, although "the loss or desolation of the provinces, from the ocean to the Alps, impaired the glory and greatness of Rome," the economic foundation of that greatness "was irretrievably destroyed by the separation of Africa."[61] As Adam Smith also observed, this unfavorable balance of trade between Italy and the provinces, under which Italy was free of taxes, had produced an inequity that was both economic and political.[62] Augustus introduced an excise tax; Caracalla "crushed alike every part of the empire" by his increase of inheritance taxes; and under Diocletian, everyone regardless of ideology regarded "the public impositions, and particularly the land-tax and capitation, as the intolerable and increasing grievance of their own times."[63]

A function both of this military decadence and of this financial exhaustion was the growth of what we today would call "bureaucracy." The English word does not seem to antedate the nineteenth century and may have come from French, but the phenomenon is older and more universal. The seventeenth chapter of the *Decline and Fall,* which is devoted primarily to the "Political System of Constantine, and his Successors," contains Gibbon's most comprehensive review of the imperial bureaucracy.[64] It reveals his own grasp of organizational behavior and of the mechanics of administering a vast administrative structure, and it bears examination as a case study in bureaucratic continuity and change; but like most of the book, it remains subordinate to "our constant attention to that great object," of "the general history of the Decline and Fall of the monarchy."[65] In keeping with that object, he was especially interested in the evolutionary process as a consequence of which the Roman bureaucracy, together with the Roman army and the Roman system of taxation, came to manifest the symptoms of "immoderate greatness." From his earlier comments on the taxes of the empire, it comes as no surprise that this should appear most explicitly in his description of that bureau:

The extraordinary title of *count of the sacred largesses* [the Latin title was *comes sacrarum largitionum*] was bestowed on the treasurer-general of the revenue, with the intention perhaps of inculcating that every payment flowed from the voluntary bounty of the monarch. To conceive the almost infinite detail of the annual and daily expense of the civil and military administration in every part of a great empire would exceed the powers of the most vigorous imagination. The actual account employed several hundred persons, distributed into eleven different offices, which were artfully contrived to examine and control their respective operations.

But Gibbon was interested not only in how all of this served the aggrandizement of the imperial office, but in how it tended to acquire a life and momentum of its own:

The multitude of these agents had a natural tendency to increase; and it was more than once thought expedient to dismiss to their native homes the useless supernumeraries, who, deserting their honest labours, had pressed with too much eagerness into the lucrative profession of the finances.[66]

Eventually, therefore, the resentment and distrust created by such a bureaucracy provoked a backlash against the empire and the emperor, for, in Gibbon's aphorism, "the prince who refuses to be the judge, instructs his people to consider him as the accomplice, of his ministers."[67]

Superficially, all of this might seem to have little to do with the triumph either of barbarism or of religion. Yet for Gibbon that would appear to have been the very point of his autopsy. "The spectator, who casts a mournful view over the ruins of ancient Rome," he commented, "is tempted to accuse the memory of the Goths and Vandals, for the mischief which they had neither leisure, nor power, nor perhaps inclination, to perpetrate." The etiology of the fatal disease lay far deeper: "the destruction which undermined the foundations of those massy fabrics was prosecuted, slowly and silently, during a period of ten centuries."[68] Thus "the principal and immediate cause of the fall of the Western Empire of Rome" may have been the presence of the Goths, who "after the defeat of Valens, *never* abandoned the Roman territory";[69] but that was not the fundamental cause. Rather, as Shakespeare has another Roman say,

> Men at some time are masters of their fates:
> The fault, dear Brutus, is not in our stars,
> But in ourselves, that we are underlings.[70]

Nor was this a matter of the morality of one or another individual, even of one or another emperor; "the effects of personal valour," Gibbon commented in describing Attila the Hun, "are so inconsiderable, except in poetry or romance, that victory, even among the Barbarians, must depend on the degree of skill with which the passions of the multitude are combined and guided for the service of a single man."[71] It was the loss of the capacity for such guidance and leadership that disclosed the fatal flaw of "immoderate great-ness" and caused for individual emperors and eventually for the empire as such "the rapid and perpetual transitions from the cottage to the throne, and from the throne to the grave."[72]

As Gibbon had already put it at about a tenth of the way into his narrative, "the form was still the same, but the animating health and vigour were fled."[73] Far earlier than that, in the third paragraph of the very first chapter, he had commented on the "valuable leg-acy" contained in the testament of the emperor Augustus, "the advice of confining the empire within those limits which nature seemed to have placed as its permanent bulwarks and bounda-ries."[74] In its literal meaning, this "moderate system" referred to geographical limits and to political boundaries as a key to Roman "greatness," but the empire had been able to thrive only so long as it had observed the limits of a "moderate system" not only geo-graphically, but politically and economically, morally and reli-giously. But, as Gibbon sadly observed, "in the prosecution of a favourite scheme, the best of men, satisfied with the rectitude of their intentions, are subject to forget the bounds of moderation."[75] Small wonder, then, that eventually the Romans "should presume to enlarge an empire whose ancient limits they were incapable of defending."[76]

"The natural and inevitable result of immoderate greatness"; "the triumph of barbarism and religion"; "crimes, follies, and mis-fortunes"; a crisis of leadership—these and similar themes in Gib-bon's *Decline and Fall* have perhaps been summarized best in the phrase "failure of nerve." It was given currency by one of the great classical scholars of the twentieth century, Gilbert Murray, Regius Professor of Greek at Oxford and translator of Greek drama, in a book originally published in 1912 as *Four Stages of Greek Religion* and revised in 1925 as *Five Stages of Greek Religion*. But the phrase itself came, as Murray tells us in his preface, from Professor J. B. Bury, editor of Gibbon's *Decline and Fall of the Roman Empire*. "We were discussing," Murray recalled, "the change that took place in Greek thought between, say, Plato and the Neo-Platonists, or even be-tween Aristotle and Posidonius, and which is seen at its highest power in the Gnostics." In planning his chapter about this change, he continued, "I had been calling it a rise of asceticism, or mysti-cism, or religious passion, or the like, when my friend corrected me." "It is not a rise," J. B. Bury insisted; "it is a fall or failure of something, a sort of failure of nerve."[77] And "The Failure of Nerve" is what the fourth chapter and fourth stage of *Five Stages of Greek Religion* became. The phrase itself, then, does not come from the *Decline and Fall* itself, but from the most learned of its editors; yet it is hard to imagine that Edward Gibbon would not have made it his own.

Part Four

LOSS AND GAIN

If the decline of the Roman empire was hastened by the conversion of Constantine, his victorious religion broke the violence of the fall, and mollified the ferocious temper of the conquerors.

CHAPTER 8

The Terrestrial Glory of an Excellent Empire

The most important work of thought and literature to come out of the social triumph of the ancient church was certainly Augustine's *City of God.* Of the "two hundred and thirty-two separate books, or treatises, on theological subjects, besides a complete exposition of the psalter and the gospel, and a copious magazine of epistles and homilies" that had been preserved, the *City of God* was one of the two works of Augustine with which Edward Gibbon felt able to claim "personal acquaintance," but this acquaintance had been enough to convince him that Augustine "possessed a strong, capacious, argumentative mind."[1] In his own chapter on the sack of Rome by Alaric, Gibbon commented on Augustine's treatment of the same events, including his statements about Alaric's respect for the shrine of Peter:

The learned work, concerning the *City of God,* was professedly composed by St. Augustin, to justify the ways of Providence in the destruction of the Roman greatness. He celebrates with peculiar satisfaction this memorable triumph of Christ; and insults his adversaries by challenging them to produce some similar example of a town taken by storm in which the fabulous gods of antiquity had been able to protect either themselves or their deluded votaries.[2]

Unfair though it is in many ways both to Augustine's intent and to the tone of the work itself, this passage is evidence for the dominant place occupied by Augustine's *City of God* throughout the history of reflection about the social triumph of the ancient church and the decline and fall of the Roman Empire. There is much to be said for the judgment that one of the several purposes Gibbon had in mind when writing his *Decline and Fall* was what might be called an anti-apologetic apologetic, to refute, by means of a description of "the triumph of barbarism and religion" over the Roman Empire, the Augustinian celebration of the triumph of religion over both the barbarism of the invaders and the barbarism of the Roman Empire.

In any full-length scholarly monograph treating Augustine's *City of God* exclusively, rather than several of the Christian responses to the fall of Rome together with Edward Gibbon's revisions of them, it would be necessary to consider at some length Augustine's literary and theological relation to at least one of his predecessors and to at least one of his successors in this enterprise of Christian apologetics. The Spanish priest Orosius had written such a response entitled *History Against the Pagans* and had dedicated it to Augustine. Recognizing on the basis of Orosius that "it is the plan and study of the Christian apologist to magnify the calamities of the pagan world," including such natural calamities as floods, Gibbon exclaimed: "How many interesting facts might Orosius have inserted in the vacant space which is devoted to pious nonsense!"[3] But he did draw on Orosius for some interesting data about the events of the fourth century, including some statistics about naval warfare that he found unbelievable, as well as the graphic description of the "wretched cottages, scattered amidst the ruins of magnificent cities, [that] still recorded the rage of the barbarians" in the third century.[4] It was likewise from Orosius that Gibbon took the text of the "pacific views" expressed by "the brave Adolphus," the brother-in-law and successor of Alaric, which, if accurately reported by Orosius who claims to have heard them in person, constitute a remarkable commentary on the political philosophy and historical sophistication of the Gothic invaders:

In the full confidence of valour and victory I once aspired to change the face of the universe; to obliterate the name of Rome; to erect on its ruins the dominion of the Goths; and to acquire, like Augustus, the immortal fame of the founder of a new empire. By repeated experiments I was gradually convinced that laws are essentially necessary to maintain and regulate a well-constituted state, and that the fierce untractable humour of the Goths was incapable of bearing the salutary yoke of laws and civil government. From that moment I proposed to myself a different object of glory and ambition; and it is now my sincere wish that the gratitude of future ages should acknowledge, the merit of a stranger who employed the sword of the Goths, not to subvert, but to restore and maintain, the prosperity of the Roman empire.[5]

Summarizing recent scholarship on the relation between Augustine and Orosius, Peter Brown observes: "Orosius, despite his courtesy to Augustine, had reached his own conclusions, that were very different from Augustine's. Augustine shared neither Orosius's interest in palliating the barbarian invasions, nor his basic assumptions on the providential role of the Roman Empire. The *History* that had been dedicated to him joined the many books of his contemporaries that Augustine pointedly ignored."[6]

In a full-length study it would likewise be necessary to draw out in some detail a comparison between Augustine's *City of God* and the book *On the Governance of God* by Salvian of Marseilles, which appeared some years after Augustine's death. Gibbon cited from "Salvian, the preacher of the age," the judgment that "the peculiar vices of each country were collected in the sink of Carthage," in particular the "abominations" of an "impious contempt of monks and the shameless practice of unnatural lusts."[7] It was also in a footnote on Salvian's *On the Governance of God*—but one that probably included Augustine's *City of God* in its judgment—that Gibbon made the wry comment: "Salvian has attempted to explain the moral government of the Deity; a task which may be readily performed by supposing that the calamities of the wicked are *judgments,* and those of the righteous, *trials.*"[8] Gibbon's editor, J. B. Bury, devoted one of his many scholarly appendices to Orosius and Salvian: of the former Bury writes that "his spirit is that of a narrow-minded provincial bigot, but he has some very important entries for the history of his own time"; and concerning the latter he says, correctly, that "the importance of the work of Salvian . . . for the state of the Empire in the fourth century is not adequately realized by Gibbon."

More puzzling and problematical, however, is Bury's subsequent comment that "Augustine's answer [to the problem of the decline and fall of Rome] was merely negative: the evils which had come upon Rome were not the effect of the introduction of Christianity."[9] Such a reading of the *City of God* vastly oversimplifies its fundamental thesis about the ambiguous combination of loss and gain involved in the fall of Rome. That combination of loss and gain was what enabled Augustine simultaneously to make his "negative" judgments about the Roman Empire and to recognize what he called "the terrestrial glory of that most excellent empire" as a genuine good, indeed a divine reward to the Romans.[10] In that connection it would perhaps also have been appropriate for Bury to add that the contrasts between Augustine and Salvian are due not only to the theological differences that the monks of Marseilles at just this time were having with Augustine's legacy, as those differences are reflected in the so-called Semi-Pelagian controversies of the fifth century,[11] but to a difference between the audiences of the two works. Salvian was writing with an eye principally on his Christian readers of the generation or two after Augustine, and he used *On the Governance of God* as a tract for the times to point a moral for believers who seemed inclined to ignore their social and political responsibilities and who appeared to him to be using the calamities of the pagan empire as an excuse for their own indifference.

It is, however, necessary to pay more adequate attention to Augustine's connections with the two other Christian responses to the fall of Rome being considered here, that of Jerome and those of Eusebius-Socrates-Sozomen, for they do provide a context within which to read the *City of God*. Although the *City of God* has often been described as Augustine's venture into the field of universal world history, the closest he actually comes to such an enterprise is the essay that forms Book Eighteen. After reviewing what he had been doing for the first seventeen books, Augustine recalled his promise at the very beginning of the work not only to make "the glorious city of God my theme," but also "as the plan of this work we have undertaken requires, and as occasion offers, [to] speak as well of the earthly city, which, though it be mistress of the nations, is itself ruled by its lust for ruling."[12] Or, as he now formulated it, he had "promised to write of the rise, progress, and appointed end of the two cities, one of which is God's, the other of which this world's, in which so far as mankind is concerned, the former is now a stranger." But he admitted that he had spent most of those first seventeen books on the city of God, and only now did he finally get around "to doing what I have heretofore passed by, and to showing, so far as seems necessary, how that other city has run its course."[13]

In turning at last to world history, Augustine drew on a variety of earlier writers. Throughout the *City of God* there are quotations from the Roman historian Sallust, who makes an occasional but colorful appearance in Gibbon[14] and whose book, *The War Against Catiline*, Augustine quoted also at the beginning of Book Eighteen,[15] and from the historian and philosopher Varro, for whose lost work, the *Antiquities,* Augustine is perhaps our principal source.[16] But for the epitome of world history in Book Eighteen, Jerome and Eusebius were his two chief Christian sources. Augustine himself refers here, for example, to "our writers of chronicles—first Eusebius, and afterwards Jerome."[17] Then he cites the two authors together, either by name or simply as "the chronicles."[18] That is not to say that Augustine uses Eusebius and Jerome uncritically. At one point, for example, he calls them to account for an "error in negligently copying the works of others" on the chronology of the minor prophets of the Old Testament.[19] It is also possible that the *Chronographies* of Sextus Julius Africanus—the third-century Christian author whose name Gibbon linked with that of Origen as "possess[ing] a very considerable share of the learning of their times"[20]—may have been used by Augustine directly, as it was by Eusebius, even though Augustine did not cite him by name as he did Eusebius and Jerome.

Augustine's dependence on Eusebius and Jerome for his chronologies and other historical information is less important here than is his implicit critique of the historical and theological interpretations that each had presented of the events associated with the fall of Rome and the triumph of the church. Augustine's relation with Jerome has long fascinated students of both men. Together with Augustine's separate treatise *On Lying,* what Gibbon called "the peevish dispute of St. Jerom and St. Augustin"[21] about lying and about the circumstances, if any, under which it was permissible not to tell the truth, has had since the Middle Ages an "impact" that can only be described as "immense."[22] In the present context the principal issue is Augustine's attitude toward Jerome's work as a biblical commentator. Jerome's acknowledged superiority in the areas of philology and textual study was often helpful to Augustine in his own exposition of the Scriptures, especially of the Old Testament. Augustine, for most of his life, had (to paraphrase Ben Jonson's familiar comment about Shakespeare) "small Greek, and less Hebrew." Clearly he admired—and also envied—Jerome's linguistic erudition. Therefore when, here in the *City of God,* he took up Jerome's *Commentary on Daniel,* he was obliged to pay his respect to it as a book "written with a proper measure of erudition and care."[23]

In the actual interpretation of the Book of Daniel, as well as of Ezekiel and of the Revelation of Saint John, however, Augustine broke quite sharply with the apocalypticism, even the "chastened apocalypticism" to which Jerome's view of the decline and fall of the Roman Empire had given voice. The break is clearly visible in what Augustine did with the words of 2 Thess. 2:7: "The mystery of iniquity is already at work; only let the one who is now holding it back do so until he is out of the way." As has been noted earlier, it was the opinion of most early Christian interpreters that this was a clear reference to the Roman Empire, which would endure until the time came for the appearance of Antichrist, the man of sin and son of perdition, who would sit in the place of God and exalt himself above all that is called God. That view determined the meaning they put not only on the sack of Rome itself but on the historical function of the pagan Caesars, as can be seen from the description of Diocletian by Lactantius.[24] Prophesying the coming of Antichrist in connection with the impending fall of Rome, Lactantius, whom Gibbon praised for a Christianity "of a moral rather than of a mysterious cast,"[25] described in detail the "unnatural phenomena" that would accompany the devastation of the world.[26] "Therefore," Lactantius wrote in summary, "as the end of the world approaches, the condition of human affairs must undergo a change, and through the prevalence of wickedness become worse." "My mind dreads to relate this," he continued. But it was evident to him, presumably on the basis of the qualification about "the one who now holds it back," that "the cause of this desolation and confusion will be this: The Roman name, by which the world is now ruled, will be taken away from the earth, and the government return to Asia; and the East will again bear rule, and the West be returned to servitude,"[27] after all of which the end would come.

Augustine was not so sure. "I frankly acknowledge," he wrote in Book Twenty of the *City of God,* "that I do not know what [the apostle Paul] means" in the use of the term "the one who now holds it back."[28] The Thessalonians had apparently not needed any glosses to identify for them Paul's specific historical point of reference; but "we who do not have their knowledge wish to understand what the apostle was referring to, and are not able to do so even with pains." This much was clear and beyond the variations of exegetical opinion: "That Christ will not come to judge the quick and the dead unless Antichrist, his adversary, first comes to seduce those who are dead in soul." Though he was not sure about the specific interpretation, he was willing "nevertheless to cite the human conjectures that I have heard or read." The first of these "conjectures" was, quite naturally, the identification of the Roman

Empire as "the one who now holds it back" and the one whose continuance was the force restraining the appearance of Antichrist and the end of history. He was willing to call this interpretation "not absurd," perhaps out of deference to the eminent interpreters who held it, but it is obvious from his own handling of it that he found it considerably less than satisfying.

He was evidently drawn much more to another and more subtle interpretation of these words, as a reference to the false Christians who belonged to the external and visible fellowship of the empirical church. As far as both the other members of the church and its enemies were able to tell, they were genuine members of the church. Yet they did not in fact belong to the true and eternal church as it would exist for eternity—and as therefore it already existed now, in the eternal "now" of the knowledge and presence of God. As long as these inauthentic members adhered to the organizational structure and sacramental fellowship of the church without in fact belonging to its soul (since they had not been predestined for permanent participation in its glory), the end of the world would not come, for the end was the sifting of humanity and of the church, the separation of the wheat and the tares prophesied by the parable of Jesus about the harvest of the Last Judgment (Matt. 13:24–30). Against the Donatists of North Africa, whom he accused of trying to form premature judgments in order to achieve a morally pure church now, Augustine declared: "The harvest is the end of the world, not the era of [their founder] Donatus!"[29] In that sense the hypocrites and false members within the institutional church were the ones "who now hold it back." Conflating the words from 2 Thessalonians 2 and from the epistles of John in the usual manner, but as usual adding his own twist, Augustine suggested:

As therefore there went out from the church many heretics, whom John calls "many antichrists," at that time [of the apostles] prior to the end, so in the end they shall go out who do not belong to Christ, but to that Antichrist [even though they now apparently do belong to Christ, because they belong externally to the church]; and then he shall be revealed.[30]

But even this interpretation, which was much more compatible with the view of the church articulated not only in the *City of God* but in his writings generally, did not completely satisfy Augustine as a definitive exegesis of this particular passage, and he finally had to leave its meaning in doubt.

What was not in doubt, for Augustine, was the error of the

millennialist definition of the kingdom of God that so often underlay Christian apocalypticism. Millennialism derived its name from
the prophecy in the twentieth chapter of the Book of Revelation (v.
6) that the saints "will reign with [Christ] a thousand years." "Ri-
diculous fancies" was only one of the terms Augustine used for such
a definition.[31] In a lengthy excursus contained appropriately in
Book Twenty of the *City of God,* Augustine examined various interpretations of the twentieth chapter of the Book of Revelation, concluding that it was not, as primitive Christian millennialism had
read it, a description of the end game in the drama of human history,
but that "it is about this kingdom militant, in which the conflict
with the enemy is still going on . . . that the Apocalypse speaks."[32]
Thus, in the striking phrase of Hermann Reuter, "the millennium
was transformed from an eschatological fact to a period of church
history."[33] In that sense Augustine could be said to have lined up
with Eusebius and against Jerome.

Yet in locating the thousand years' rule of the saints immanently
within this present history, Augustine was not in any simplistic way
adopting the Eusebian interpretation of the fall of Rome as the
social triumph of the ancient church. As in the case of his difference
from Jerome, it is instructive here to look at a specific element in his
interpretation: the Christian emperors Constantine and Theodosius.
Augustine did indeed join Eusebius, Socrates, and Sozomen in
praising Constantine as a worshiper of the true God, and with them
he attributed the political successes and military victories of this
Christian emperor to the action of God.[34] But he said all of this only
after he had pointed out a few paragraphs earlier that the God who
ruled human history had granted power not only to the noble
Augustus but also to the cruel Nero, and that "he who gave it to
the Christian Constantine gave it also to the apostate Julian" in
accordance with his sovereign but hidden will.[35] As for the Christian emperor Theodosius, of whom Socrates and Sozomen spoke so
effusively, Augustine, after reciting various evidences of the emperor's devotion to Christ and to the orthodoxy of the church that
made him "a model Christian prince,"[36] climaxed his own panegyric, by contrast with those of his Greek contemporaries in Constantinople, with a description of the ultimate proof of Theodosius's
piety: his willingness, in the year 390, to prostrate himself in public
penance before the discipline of the church after he had sinned,
when, in Gibbon's words, "the rigid Ambrose commanded Theo-

dosius to retire before the rails, and taught him to know the difference between a king and a priest"[37]—an incident about which Augustine would have known directly from his own "father in Christ," Bishop Ambrose of Milan.[38]

Thus Augustine found himself in the position of not being able either to condemn Old Rome altogether or to commend it unequivocally. He paid tribute to Cato both for his personal virtue, which Augustine judged to have come closest in his time to the true definition of virtue, and for his contribution to the Roman Republic.[39] God had, according to Augustine, granted to the Romans "the terrestrial glory of that most excellent empire" as a reward for their virtue.[40] This was not the reward granted to the elect in the city of God, but it was a genuine reward nonetheless. And in the peroration to Book Two of the *City of God* he called upon the Romans to "purge and perfect" their virtues by turning to the true God and forsaking their idols.[41] On the other hand, it was the worship of these idols and the consequent excesses of ambition and vainglory that had vitiated the peace and justice to which Rome claimed to be devoted; and if justice was undermined, what was a kingdom but a glorified robber band?[42] The swing of the pendulum at work in the decline and fall of the Roman Empire, in God's conferral of imperial power on Constantine the pious and then on Julian the apostate, was for Augustine a characteristic of the historical process. Within this historical process, the relation between the "celestial glory" of the city of God and the "terrestrial glory" of the city of earth was a dialectical one. Despite his Hegelian orientation (or perhaps even because of it), Heinrich Scholz was quite correct in entitling a central part of his book on Augustine "the dialectic of history."[43] The "two cities," Augustine wrote, "are entangled together in this world, and intermixed until the Last Judgment brings about their separation," and their history together was a "checkered" one.[44] There was likewise a dialectic within the history of the earthly city itself, as was evident in the history of Rome.

But Augustine's historical dialectic was no less visible in his description of the city of God than it was in his interpretation of the city of earth. While "the terrestrial glory" of the Roman Empire served as the concrete historical embodiment for the "city of earth," Augustine did not, throughout most of the work, provide a similar empirical referent for the "city of God." Then in Book Twenty, "suddenly and unexpectedly" as Scholz says,[45] there comes the identification of it with the church. Or, to be utterly precise, Augustine identifies the church here as the "kingdom of Christ" and does so six times in chapter 9 of Book Twenty alone. It was, moreover, the empirical church—in fact, the hierarchical church—to which the bishop of Hippo attached this identification. Expanding the exegesis of Revelation 20 cited earlier, Augustine averred that this chapter "does not refer to the Last Judgment, but to the thrones of the rulers and to the rulers themselves by whom the church is now being governed," that is, to the bishops to whom Christ had given the power of binding and loosing sins.[46]

Yet that equation of the city of God with the institutional church was only one pole of the dialectic, for the church in the ultimate sense was, in the *City of God* as in Augustine's other works, the New Jerusalem, the company of the elect, hidden from human gaze and known only to God. To this true and ultimate church belonged some who were not now a part of empirical, organized Christendom. Conversely, others who were now pillars of the institutional church and of its hierarchy were in fact not members of the true church in the mysterious knowledge and inscrutable predestination of God. There is an eloquent paragraph on this paradox and dialectic near the end of the very first book of the *City of God:*

Let these and similar answers (if any fuller and fitter answers can be found) be given to their enemies by the redeemed family of Christ the Lord, and by the pilgrim city of Christ the King. But let this city bear in mind that among her enemies there lie hidden those who are destined to be fellow citizens, so that she may not think it a fruitless labor to bear what they inflict as enemies until they become confessors of the faith. So long, too, as she is a stranger in the world, the city of God has in her communion, and bound to her by the sacraments, some who will not eternally dwell in the lot of the saints.[47]

Both poles of this dialectic, the tension between the church as historical and the church as eternal,[48] had been worked out especially in Augustine's controversy with the Donatists of North Africa, in which he defended the institutional church and its ministry and sacraments by pointing beyond it to the eternal church of the elect.

Both poles of the dialectic have likewise appeared and reappeared since Augustine. Not only because of its literary roots in Eusebius and Jerome, but especially because of its subtlety and depth, Augustine's *City of God,* with its interpretation of the loss and gain in the fall of Rome and the triumph of the church, has been the primary form in which both of those other versions of the triumph have been transmitted to subsequent centuries in the history of Western thought. The *City of God* has also been the proximate source from which both the apocalypticism associated with Jerome and the triumphalism associated with Eusebius have repeatedly taken their rise. The most influential species of apocalypticism in the later Middle Ages, that associated with the name of Joachim of Fiore, presented itself as a new reading of the history of the city of God, in which "Angel Pope and Papal Antichrist," to cite the title of a recent study of the question,[49] once more made Rome the key to the understanding of the mysterious purposes of God within human and ecclesiastical history. At the same time, what has been called "political Augustinianism"[50] represented at least in part the attempt to draw out of Augustine's *City of God* a consistent political theory; we have it on the authority of Charlemagne's biographer that "he took great pleasure in the books of Saint Augustine and especially in those which are called *The City of God.*"[51]

Therefore when Edward Gibbon took upon himself the task of writing a history of the decline and fall of the Roman Empire, the dominant tradition—or rather traditions—of understanding "the terrestrial glory of an excellent empire" had come from Augustine. Augustine had not been a historian, not even in the sense that Jerome, author of a book called *Lives of Illustrious Men,* had been, much less in the sense that Eusebius, Socrates, Sozomen, and Theodoret, each of them the author of a book called *Ecclesiastical History,* had been. But by the eighteenth century, critical history had come of age as a discipline, so that, as Gibbon said as he began his work, "the temper, as well as knowledge, of a modern historian require a more sober and accurate knowledge."[52] That requirement included a more accurate and a more sober knowledge both of the loss and of the gain entailed in the decline and fall.

CHAPTER 9

The Inestimable Gifts
of Roman Civilization

The fundamental difference between an interpretation of the decline and fall of the Roman Empire that looks upon it as the social triumph of the ancient church and one that regards it as the triumph of barbarism and religion lies in the comparative values attached to the loss and to the gain. If Augustine, in Gibbon's words, "celebrates with peculiar satisfaction this memorable triumph of Christ,"[1] Augustine's "satisfaction" was nevertheless tempered by his recognition of what he himself called "the terrestrial glory of that most excellent empire";[2] and it is impossible to avoid the question of what his feelings must have been as he lay dying in 430 as the Vandals stood at the gates of Hippo celebrating, if not the triumph of barbarism and religion, then certainly the triumph of barbarism. Gibbon, in turn, despite his profound resentment at how a victorious Christianity had "insulted human nature in the sages of antiquity"[3] and his constant use of such words as "mournful" to describe the irreparable loss, was not insensible of the positive gain that accompanied it.

At the conclusion of the "General Observations on the Fall of the Roman Empire in the West" appended to the thirty-eighth chapter of the *Decline and Fall,* therefore, he expressed his credo, though tinged with more than a little irony as most of Gibbon's credo was, that "the experience of four thousand years should enlarge our hopes, and diminish our apprehensions." While it had to be admitted that "we cannot determine to what height the human species may aspire in their advances towards perfection" and while he had learned from the history of Rome that such advances toward perfection had never been unilinear, he did advance it as a safe assumption "that no people, unless the face of nature is changed, will relapse into their original barbarism." From that assumption he proceeded to an enumeration of some of the advances that had gone beyond the "original barbarism" and concluded, once again with considerable irony:

Since the first discovery of the arts, war, commerce, and religious zeal have diffused, among the savages of the Old and New World, these inestimable gifts: they have been successively propagated; they can never be lost. We may therefore acquiesce in the pleasing conclusion that every age of the world has increased, and still increases, the real wealth, the happiness, the knowledge, and perhaps the virtue, of the human race.[4]

Elsewhere, too, he spoke about these "inestimable gifts." In the autograph annotations to the first paragraph of the first chapter of the *Decline and Fall*, which are preserved in the British Museum, Gibbon revised the concluding words—"to deduce the most important circumstances of its decline and fall: a revolution which will ever be remembered, and is still felt by the nations of the earth"[5]— to read instead: "to prosecute the decline and fall of the empire of Rome: of whose language, religion and laws the impression will be long preserved in our own and the neighbouring countries of Europe."[6] That same triad appears also in the main body of the work itself, although in the sequence "the laws, the language, and the religion of the Romans,"[7] which can stand as a convenient summary of his appreciation for the "inestimable gifts" of Roman civilization to medieval and modern culture.

Gibbon held the achievement of Roman *law* in high esteem and was "not afraid to affirm that the brief composition of the Decemvirs surpasses in genuine value the libraries of Grecian philosophy," though he recognized that this primitive "jurisprudence . . . was polished and improved in the seventh century of the city by the alliance of Grecian philosophy."[8] The ambiguous relation of this achievement to the decline and fall of Rome made itself visible early in his account: between the description of how "the fine theory of a republic insensibly vanished" and the conclusion of the following paragraph, that "posterity . . . justly considered [Severus] as the principal author of the decline of the Roman empire," he observed that at this very time "the Roman jurisprudence, having closely united itself with the system of monarchy, was supposed to have attained its full maturity and perfection."[9] Although there was an occasional emperor such as Tacitus (ruler for just over half a year in 275–276) who in the republican tradition "considered that national council [the senate] as the author, and himself as the subject, of the laws," even he was unsuccessful in dealing with "the wounds which Imperial pride, civil discord, and military violence had inflicted on the constitution."[10]

Those wounds infected the theory and the practice of Roman jurisprudence, "some of [whose] noblest regulations . . . have been suffered to expire."[11] Yet the ambiguity continued, for the "arduous but indispensable" achievement of codifying the Roman law stood as an "everlasting monument" to the emperor Justinian.[12] Despite his own "diffidence" about entering a field of scholarship "which has exhausted so many learned lives and clothed the walls of such spacious libraries," Gibbon did feel qualified to undertake the examination of this inestimable gift, precisely because he was "attached to no party, interested only for the truth and candour of history, and directed by the most temperate and skilful guides." The resulting chapter, number forty-four in the *Decline and Fall,* is, as Bury correctly says, "still not only famous, but admired by jurists as a brief and brilliant exposition of the principles of Roman law." "To say that it is worthy of the subject," Bury continues, "is the best tribute that can be paid to it."[13]

Gibbon was thus compelled to pay his own tribute to Justinian, the Christian emperor in Constantinople, New Rome, for accomplishing what the pagan Romans in Old Rome had themselves not been able to accomplish during either the republic or the empire. "If Caesar had achieved the reformation of the Roman law," Gibbon thought, "his creative genius, enlightened by reflection and study, would have given the world a pure and original system of jurisprudence"; Justinian's codification, by contrast, was "a tesselated pavement of antique and costly, but too often of incoherent, fragments."[14] He gave mixed grades to the legislation of the Christian emperors overall. To an eighteenth-century protagonist of the Enlightenment, intolerance was the characteristic of the legislation that most clearly demonstrated a decline from the heights of classical Roman law. According to the famous description of Roman tolerance in the second chapter of the *Decline and Fall,* "the various modes of worship which prevailed in the Roman world were all considered by the people as equally true; by the philosopher as equally false; and by the magistrate as equally useful"; "and thus," in pagan Rome, "toleration produced not only mutual indulgence, but even religious concord."[15] The persecutions of the church under various of the emperors indicated that this "religious policy of the ancient world seems to have assumed a more stern and intolerant character, to oppose the progress of Christianity."[16] Therefore, as Gibbon observed on the basis of the Venerable Bede, "the first missionaries who preached the gospel to the Barbarians appealed to the evidence of reason, and claimed the benefit of toleration."[17]

Once Christianity had triumphed, however, the situation was gradually reversed—only gradually, for although Constantine "advanced, by slow and cautious steps, to undermine the irregular and decayed fabric of polytheism," he meanwhile decreed that "those who still refuse to open their eyes to the celestial light may freely enjoy their temples and their fancied gods."[18] By a paradox that has continued to intrigue historians,[19] the policies and legislation of Constantine proscribed and persecuted the various Christian heresies far more fiercely than they did the remnants of paganism. Near the end of the same century, the emperor Theodosius formalized into positive law much of Constantine's action against heresy.[20] It was also in the reign of Theodosius, however, under the influence of Christian bishops, that "two specious principles of religious jurisprudence were established." These principles were: "*that* the magistrate is, in some measure, guilty of the crimes which he neglects to prohibit or to punish; and *that* the idolatrous worship of fabulous deities and real daemons is the most abominable crime against the supreme majesty of the Creator." On this basis paganism was destroyed in law and finally in fact, "and the temples of the Roman world were subverted, about sixty years after the conversion of Constantine."[21] Meanwhile the legislation of the Christian emperors, beginning with the edict of Milan, extended to the institutions and property of the church a variety of legal protections and privileges, among which some of the most important were the "legal prerogatives, which secured and dignified the sacerdotal character" by granting the clergy immunity from prosecution in the civil courts (the origins of "benefit of clergy").[22]

By another of those same "legal prerogatives," however, "the ancient privilege of sanctuary was transferred to the Christian temples." Thereby, as Gibbon recognized, "the rash violence of despotism was suspended by the mild interposition of the church."[23] The mild interposition of the church made itself felt as well in other areas of Roman law, especially family law, where rash violence had been sanctioned. Gibbon had criticism for Constantine's laws prohibiting rape, which, he commented, "were dictated with very little indulgence for the most amiable weaknesses of human nature."[24] But his judgment was different when he came to the ancient Roman principle of *patria potestas,* which had been "instituted or confirmed by Romulus himself" and had been "inscribed on the fourth table of the Decemvirs." *Patria potestas* gave to the father as head of the family virtually absolute power of life and death, especially over the newborn.[25] Already in the legislation of Constantine, that power was significantly curtailed by his edict against "the horrid practice, so familiar to the ancients, of exposing or murdering their new-born infants." Constantine's edict against the exposure of infants, which is one of the less frequently noticed precedents for the prohibition of abortion in both canon and civil law, directed that there be public assistance for parents whose poverty was causing them to expose their children. Gibbon concluded that "the law, though it may merit some praise, served rather to display than to alleviate the public distress."[26]

The inestimable gift of Roman law had nevertheless degenerated through "the decline of Roman jurisprudence," especially during the two centuries of Christian rule from Constantine to Justinian.[27] When it was transmitted to subsequent centuries during the time that the various law codes of the barbarians were evolving, moreover, it degenerated still further. Gibbon set forth in considerable detail the major characteristics of these barbarian codes as a group.[28] Although a comparison of Roman and barbarian law would "ascribe to the Romans the superior advantages, not only of science and reason, but of humanity and justice," it had to be granted that "the laws of the Barbarians were adapted to their wants and desires, their occupations, and their capacity." Such institutions of barbarian law as wergild ("the moderate fine which has been ascertained as the price of blood") and trial by combat (because "a warlike people . . . could not believe that a brave man deserved to suffer, or that a coward deserved to live"), though perhaps offensive to Roman legal and modern moral sensitivities, meant in fact, in Gibbon's phrase, that "the law, which now favours the rich, then yielded to the strong." He then went on to describe in particular several of the barbarian codes and their relation to Roman jurisprudence.[29] The

Frankish law "might have been polished and improved by the civil wisdom of the Romans," but it was not; as Bury observes, "there is little trace of Roman, and none of Christian, influence in the Lex Salica" of the Franks.[30] In Spain, after a period during which the Visigothic kings "indulged their subjects of Aquitain and Spain in the enjoyment of the Roman law," this was replaced by their own "code of civil and criminal jurisprudence, for the use of a great and united people." And in Britain, the laws "which the Romans had so carefully planted . . . were extirpated by their barbarian successors." Among them all, in fact, "the laws of the Lombards have been esteemed the least imperfect of the barbaric codes."

The positive contribution of the "inestimable gift" of the Latin *language* and of Roman letters was considerably less ambiguous, although no less complicated, for to Gibbon "language [is] the leading principle which unites or separates the tribes of mankind."[31] Although the Goths and some of the other barbarians who came into the Western empire may sometimes have manifested a "contempt for the Latin schools" and for the Latin language, it was also true that in general "the Barbarians were ambitious of conversing in Latin, the military idiom even of the Eastern empire."[32] Latin was in a much more parlous state as a literary language in the Eastern empire, where "Greek was the language of literature and philosophy"; "nor could," Gibbon continued, "the masters of this rich and perfect idiom be tempted to envy the borrowed learning and imitative taste of their Roman disciples." As a consequence, it was, he believed, from the reign of Justinian that "we may date the gradual oblivion of the Latin tongue" among the Byzantines, and this in spite of the anomaly that "in the lowest period of degeneracy and decay, the name of ROMANS adhered to the last fragments of the empire of Constantinople."[33] So it was that the barbarians of the West became the heirs of Latin, as an unintended, perhaps even an unwanted, byproduct of their conversion to Christianity. With their conversion "they received, at the same time, the use of letters, so essential to a religion whose doctrines are contained in a sacred book." The language of Jerome's Vulgate and of the Roman liturgy of the Mass "concealed the inestimable monuments of ancient learning." Whatever the missionaries may have intended, therefore, "the immortal productions of Virgil, Cicero, and Livy, which were accessible to the Christian barbarians, maintained a silent intercourse between the reign of Augustus and the times of Clovis and

Charlemagne."³⁴ The contrasting missionary method of the Eastern church led to opposite cultural consequences: because the missionaries from Constantinople to the Slavs, Cyril and Methodius, translated not only the Bible but also the liturgy into the language of the people, the Slavs of the East did not have the same access to Greek that Western Christians had to Latin.

The gift of Latin to Western Christian nations was in several instances even greater than that. The Roman hope that the barbarians "would be polished by time, education, and the influence of Christianity; and that their prosperity would blend with the great body of the Roman people"³⁵ was fulfilled in a special way when several of the barbarian nations eventually surrendered their native tongues to a new vernacular derived from Latin. Thus "in the space of four hundred years, the Gauls, who had encountered the arms of Caesar, were imperceptibly melted into the general mass of citizens and subjects," so that when they encountered the Franks, "their ears were astonished by the harsh and unknown sounds of the Germanic dialect"; and in turn, "the Franks, after they mingled with their Gallic subjects,"³⁶ took over their Latinate language. Summarizing the state of comparative philology in his time, Gibbon assessed the Latin heritage in various Romance languages as "the change of language" affected "the Lombards of Italy, and the Visigoths of Spain." He thought that "modern Italian has been insensibly formed by the mixture of the nations," but that in it "the principal stock of technical and familiar words is found to be of Latin derivation."³⁷ Much earlier he had already noted that "the Walachians [of present-day Romania] still preserve many traces of the Latin language, and have boasted in every age of their Roman descent."³⁸

Ironically, this very debt of various European vernaculars to the Latin language could, and sometimes did, mean the loss of contact with Latin literature. Through what Gibbon calls the "execrable practice" of using an older manuscript, with the earlier text erased, to copy a more recent work (what modern codicology calls a "palimpsest"), some of "the most beautiful compositions of genius" from classical times were destroyed, as "Sophocles or Tacitus were obliged to resign the parchment to missals, homilies, and the golden legend" of saints' lives.³⁹ Yet Gibbon knew that this was an oversimplification of the relation between Christianity and classical culture. His portrait of Pope Gregory I, for example, describes "his implacable aversion to the monuments of classic genius," but goes

A

VINDICATION

OF

SOME PASSAGES

IN THE

Fifteenth and Sixteenth Chapters

OF THE

HISTORY of the DECLINE and FALL of
the ROMAN EMPIRE.

BY THE AUTHOR.

LONDON:
PRINTED FOR W. STRAHAN; AND T. CADELL,
IN THE STRAND.
MDCCLXXIX.

Title page from Edward Gibbon's *A Vindication of Some Passages in the 15th and 16th Chapters of The History of the Decline and Fall of the Roman Empire*, London, 1779. Photo Courtesy of The Bancroft Library, University of California, Berkeley.

on to acknowledge that "the epistles of Gregory, his sermons, and his dialogues, are the work of a man who was second in erudition to none of his contemporaries."[40]

There is perhaps no prejudice in the *Decline and Fall* more violent and more pervasive than Gibbon's antipathy to monks and monasticism, expressed at the very beginning of the book in this capsule description of Rome's decline: "On that celebrated ground the first consuls deserved triumphs, their successors adorned villas, and *their* posterity have erected convents."[41] The most concentrated form of that prejudice appears in the first part of the thirty-seventh chapter, bearing the subtitle "Origin, Progress, and Effects of the Monastic Life." For a champion of toleration, it does seem less than completely tolerant to generalize that "a cruel unfeeling temper has

distinguished the monks of every age and country: their stern indifference, which is seldom mollified by personal friendship, is inflamed by religious hatred; and their merciless zeal has strenuously
administered the holy office of the Inquisition."[42] Yet in the midst
of his diatribe, Gibbon felt constrained, though not without another
such slur, to describe the inestimable gift that even monastic culture
had communicated:

The monastic studies have tended, for the most part, to darken, rather than
to dispel, the cloud of superstition. Yet the curiosity or zeal of some learned
solitaries has cultivated the ecclesiastical, and even the profane, sciences;
and posterity must gratefully acknowledge that the monuments of Greek
and Roman literature have been preserved [through copies] and multiplied
[through forgeries] by their indefatigable pens.[43]

Even that tribute to monastic culture could not stand without a final
reminder that "all the manly virtues were oppressed by the servile
and pusillanimous reign of the monks."

A special form of Latin language and literature bequeathed to
subsequent generations by the declining and falling Roman Empire
was classical rhetoric, whose noblest embodiment for Gibbon was
probably Cicero, partly because he was not only an orator but also
a philosopher.[44] That combination of what Gibbon called "the studies of philosophy and eloquence" had characterized the oratorical
tradition at its best. He referred to "the art of speaking" as "the
powerful engine of patriotism or ambition" in the pre-Christian
republics of Greece and Rome, where "the schools of rhetoric
poured forth a colony of statesmen and legislators." Rhetoric was,
therefore, an "honourable profession" when it was employed in a
righteous cause, but it could also be abused for panegyric or sophis-
try.[45] When Christianity had triumphed, it became the function of
rhetoric to equip the bishops as preachers of the gospel with the
skills they needed to communicate the Christian message. At its
worst, such communicating "harangued, without the danger of in-
terruption or reply, a submissive multitude, whose minds had been
prepared and subdued by the awful ceremonies of religion."[46] But
even episcopal rhetoric could do better than that. Thus Latin bishops carried on the tradition of Roman rhetoric. When Ambrose the
bishop preached, "the pathetic vehemence of his sermons continu-
ally inflamed the angry and seditious temper of the people of
Milan."[47] His most eminent pupil was Augustine, whose oratorical

"style," according to Gibbon, "though sometimes animated by the eloquence of passion, is usually clouded by false and affected rhetoric"; as "a professor of rhetoric," he would not have met the standards of "Cicero or Quintilian."[48] Greek bishops were more successful. Gregory Nazianzus, who was briefly patriarch of Constantinople in 381, "was distinguished by the talents of an eloquent preacher."[49] But the title "the most eloquent of the saints" was one that Gibbon reserved for another patriarch of Constantinople, John Chrysostom.[50]

More than any bishop or theologian, however, the Christian writer who seemed to Gibbon to have understood and articulated the inestimable gift of classical language, but also the gift of authentic *religion* at its best, was probably Boethius, whose "eloquence ... flattery might compare to the voice of Demosthenes or Cicero." Gibbon devoted a vignette of several pages at the end of the thirty-ninth chapter of the *Decline and Fall* to Boethius. As "the last of the Romans whom Cato or Tully [Cicero] could have acknowledged for their countryman," Boethius had known enormous worldly success: he was "prosperous in his fame and fortunes, in his public honours and private alliances, in the cultivation of science and the consciousness of virtue." All of that came crashing around his head when he was unjustly arrested and imprisoned. The work he wrote in prison, *The Consolation of Philosophy,* was, in Gibbon's estimate—and in that of the entire Middle Ages, having been translated by King Alfred, Geoffrey Chaucer, and Queen Elizabeth I, and practically memorized by Dante—"a golden volume not unworthy of the leisure of Plato or Tully." Yet, although its author had distinguished himself as a defender of Christian orthodoxy against all kinds of heresy, he consoled himself *in extremis* by what reason, speaking through Lady Philosophy, was able to do "to reconcile the perfect attributes of the Deity with the apparent disorders of his moral and physical government,"[51] without any reference to any Christian doctrine or even to the Bible.

But Roman religion at its best had been practical rather than theoretical, and the same was true of its "inestimable gift" even in its Christian form during and after the decline and fall of Rome. Gibbon's account makes that evident most forcefully of all in its treatment of what we have been calling here the crisis of Roman leadership, the loss of what he himself had called in an early chapter "that conscious superiority, either of birth or of merit, which can alone render the possession of a throne easy, and as it were natural."[52] One of the most influential factors in the decline and fall was the diversion of natural leaders who had such a "conscious superiority" from politics to religion, from the empire to the church. Not only was it assumed that the renunciation of the world by the monks had fitted them for the governance of the church,[53] but in fact the crisis was more general than that: those who were the most fitted for governance in the state were now often renouncing public life and becoming monks, priests, and bishops. The careers of Ambrose and Gregory the Great were especially striking illustrations of this trend. In 374, "before he had received the sacrament of baptism, Ambrose, to his own surprise, and to that of the world, was suddenly transformed from a governor to an archbishop." The impressive talents that he had been bringing to political administration he now placed at the service of the church as archbishop of Milan.[54] Two centuries or so later, Gregory, whose "birth and abilities had raised him to the office of praefect of the city," had all the talents of "a crafty and ambitious statesman," including "a singular mixture of simplicity and cunning, of pride and humility, of sense and superstition"; but he used all of this in the service not of the empire but of the church, first in Constantinople as "the nuncio or minister of the apostolic see" and finally as pope from 590 to 604.[55]

The most complete case study of such a diversion of leadership in the *Decline and Fall* is the portrait of "the *celestial* virtues of the great Athanasius,"[56] patriarch of Alexandria and defender of the Nicene faith. As Gibbon could not conceal his dislike for the Christian doctrine of the Trinity and his contempt for "the furious contests which the difference of a single diphthong excited between the Homoousians and the Homoiousians,"[57] no less could he suppress his admiration for Athanasius, whose "active and capacious mind" and other talents "enabled him to assume, in a moment of danger, the office of Ecclesiastical Dictator."[58] Not only was Athanasius "intrepid" and "the most sagacious of the Christian theologians," but he was a "prudent statesman."[59] His courage and skill at knowing when to bend and when to be firm, at defying his enemies even when they sat on the throne of the empire, at manipulating the populace and the leaders of both church and state to serve his political and theological purposes, and at pitting Rome and the West against Constantinople and the East—all of these political talents made him in many ways the outstanding man of his time. As a result, the *cause célèbre* of Athanasius demonstrated to foe and friend alike that at a time of political and moral decadence it was the church, not the empire, that had "revived a sense of order and freedom in the Roman government."[60] Describing and lamenting the decline of that sense of order and freedom within the body politic during the fourth century, Gibbon clearly wished that what remained of it could have been employed to preserve the integrity of the state rather than to defend the dogma of the church; almost as clearly, he saw Athanasius as perhaps the only one who could have accomplished it:

Five times was Athanasius expelled from his throne; twenty years he passed as an exile or a fugitive; and almost every province of the Roman empire was successively witness to his merit, and his sufferings in the cause of the Homoousion, which he considered as the sole pleasure and business, as the duty, and as the glory, of his life. Amidst the storms of persecution, the archbishop of Alexandria was patient of labour, jealous of fame, careless of safety; and although his mind was tainted by the contagion of fanaticism, Athanasius displayed a superiority of character and abilities, which would have qualified him, far better than the degenerate sons of Constantine, for the government of a great monarchy.[61]

If only the common weal of the Roman Empire had been able to command such "superiority of character and abilities"!

Having been "successfully propagated," these "inestimable gifts" of law, language, and religion, which had come from the empire in its decline and fall, could, Gibbon averred, "never be lost." Both the Latin language and the Christian religion "had alike degenerated from the simple purity of the Augustan, and Apostolic, age." Nevertheless, although the conversion of Constantine may have hastened the decline, it also "broke the violence of the fall, and mollified the ferocious temper of the conquerors."[62] And therefore the most inestimable gift of all from the dying empire to the modern world was, according to Gibbon's sincere and yet ironic judgment, "the union of the Christian republic," which in turn had "gradually produced the similar manners, and common jurisprudence, which have distinguished, from the rest of mankind, the independent, and even hostile, nations of modern Europe."[63] And he hoped that all of that, too, could "never be lost."

Notes

Short References

Decline and Fall   Edward Gibbon, *The History of the Decline and Fall of the Roman Empire,* ed. J. B. Bury, 7 vols. (London: Methuen, 1896–1900).

Given are Gibbon's chapter number and in parentheses the volume and page number in Bury's edition; so, for example, *Decline and Fall* 3 (1:72) means that the citation appears in chapter 3 of Gibbon and on p. 72 in volume 1 of Bury's edition.

Autobiography   Edward Gibbon, *Autobiography,* ed. Dero A. Saunders (New York: Meridian Books, 1961).

1. The Fall of Rome as Historical Paradigm

1. *Great Books of the Western World,* ed. Robert M. Hutchins and Mortimer J. Adler (Chicago: Encyclopaedia Britannica, 1952), 43:1–3; 39; 40–41.
2. *Decline and Fall,* pref. (1:v).
3. Edmund Burke, "A Letter to John Farr and John Harris, Esquires, Sheriffs of Bristol, on the Affairs of America, July 1777," in Elliott R. Barkan, ed., *Edmund Burke on the American Revolution: Selected Speeches and Letters* (New York: Harper & Row, 1966), 194–95.
4. Edmund Burke, *Reflections on the Revolution in France and on the Proceedings in Certain Societies in London Relative to that Event,* ed. Conor Cruise O'Brien (New York: Penguin Books, 1968), 371.
5. *A Dictionary of American English on Historical Principles,* ed. Sir William A. Craigie and James R. Hulbert, 4 vols. (Chicago: University of Chicago Press, 1938–1944), 3:1793.
6. Burke *Reflections on the Revolution in France* 371.
7. *Decline and Fall* 1 (1:26–27).

8. Adam Smith, *An Inquiry into the Nature and Causes of the Wealth of Nations,* 3.2, ed. Edwin Cannan, 2 vols. (Chicago: University of Chicago Press, 1976), 1:407.
9. Smith *Wealth of Nations* 1.11.1, Cannan ed. 1:167–68.
10. Smith *Wealth of Nations* 3.3, Cannan ed. 1:420–31.
11. *The Federalist,* ed. Jacob E. Cooke (Middletown, CT: Wesleyan University Press, 1961), No. 70, 473–74.
12. *Decline and Fall* 38 (4:161).
13. *The Federalist,* No. 70, Cooke ed. 473–74.
14. *The Federalist,* No. 18, Cooke ed. 110–17.
15. *The Federalist,* No. 8, Cooke ed. 47.
16. *The Federalist,* No. 41, Cooke ed. 270–71.
17. *Decline and Fall* 1 (1:14).
18. *Decline and Fall* 3 (1:72).
19. Byron, "Ode to Napoleon Bonaparte," II.
20. Alexis de Tocqueville, *Democracy in America,* ed. J. P. Mayer and Max Lerner, trans. George Lawrence (New York: Harper & Row, 1966), vol. 2, chap. 10, 430–31.
21. Quoted in George Wilson Pierson, *Tocqueville in America* (Garden City, NY: Doubleday, 1959), 375.
22. Tocqueville, *Democracy in America,* vol. 2, chap. 15, 444–45.
23. Karl Marx, *Capital: A Critique of Political Economy,* ed. Friedrich Engels, trans. Samuel Moore and Edward Aveling (New York: Random House, Modern Library, 1906), 798–99.
24. Oswald Spengler, *The Decline of the West,* trans. Charles Francis Atkinson, 2 vols. (New York: Knopf, 1981–1983), 1:1, 36, 38.
25. Hannah Arendt, *On Revolution* (New York: Viking Press, 1965), 113–14.
26. *Decline and Fall* pref. (1:xxxv).
27. *Decline and Fall* 38 (4:168–69).
28. John Thomas McNeill, Matthew Spinka, and Harold R. Willoughby, eds., *Environmental Factors in Christian History* (Chicago: University of Chicago Press, 1939), x.
29. *Decline and Fall* 71 (7:308).

2. The Social Triumph of the Ancient Church

1. Henry Chadwick, "Introduction" to *Origen: "Contra Celsum"* (Cambridge: Cambridge University Press, 1953), p. xxvi.
2. *Decline and Fall* 21 (2:395); 23–24 (2:432–519).
3. *Decline and Fall* 37 (4:68, n. 52; 4:65, n. 37).
4. *Decline and Fall* 6 (1:126, n. 3).
5. *Decline and Fall* 32 (3:374, n. 41).
6. *Decline and Fall* 14 (1:397, n. 11); 17 (2:158, n. 68); 20 (2:302, n. 41).
7. *Decline and Fall* 67 (5:124, n. 63).
8. *Decline and Fall* 47 (5:132, n. 81).
9. *Decline and Fall* 48 (5:169).
10. *Decline and Fall* 33 (5:406, n. 29).
11. *Decline and Fall* 33 (5:407, n. 30).

12. *Decline and Fall* 28 (3:211).
13. See, for example, Jaroslav Pelikan, *The Christian Tradition: A History of the Development of Doctrine*, 5 vols. (Chicago: University of Chicago Press, 1971–), 4:69–126.
14. Cyprian *On the Unity of the Church* 26.
15. Shirley Jackson Case, *The Social Triumph of the Ancient Church* (New York: Harper & Brothers, 1933), 41–93.
16. Jaroslav Pelikan, *Jesus through the Centuries: His Place in the History of Culture* (New Haven, CT: Yale University Press, 1985), 209.
17. Wayne A. Meeks, *The First Urban Christians: The Social World of the Apostle Paul* (New Haven, CT: Yale University Press, 1983).
18. See Jaroslav Pelikan, *The Preaching of Chrysostom* (Philadelphia: Fortress Press, 1967), 7–9.
19. J. N. D. Kelly, *Early Christian Creeds* (London: Longmans, Green and Co., 1950), 159.
20. *Clementine Recognitions* 8.50.
21. Celsus ap. Origen *Contra Celsum* 3.59.
22. Jaroslav Pelikan, *The Riddle of Roman Catholicism* (Nashville, TN: Abingdon Press, 1959), 21–22.
23. *Decline and Fall* 2 (1:28).
24. Adolf Harnack, *The Mission and Expansion of Christianity in the First Three Centuries*, trans. James Moffatt, intro. Jaroslav Pelikan (New York: Harper & Row, Torchbooks, 1961).
25. *Decline and Fall* 15 (2:1).
26. Pelikan *The Christian Tradition* 1:108–20.
27. Walter Rauschenbusch, *Christianizing the Social Order* (1912), in Robert T. Handy, ed., *The Social Gospel in America 1870–1920* (New York: Oxford University Press, 1966), 350.

3. The Triumph of Barbarism and Religion

1. *Decline and Fall* 71 (7:308); italics added.
2. *Decline and Fall* 71 (7:325).
3. *Autobiography* 14.
4. *Autobiography* 154.
5. *Autobiography* 154.
6. *Decline and Fall* pref. (1:v).
7. *Decline and Fall* 14 (1:441).
8. *Decline and Fall* 16 (2:138–39).
9. *Decline and Fall* 17 (2:200–201).
10. *Decline and Fall* 35 (4:479–80).
11. *Decline and Fall* 38 (4:158).
12. *Decline and Fall* 38 (4:160–69).
13. For earlier instances of this coupling of "instruction" and "amusement" as the purposes of historical study, see *Decline and Fall* 13 (1:362, 392).
14. *Decline and Fall* 48 (5:169–73).
15. *Decline and Fall* 71 (7:305–16).
16. *Autobiography* 72.

17. *Autobiography* 82.

18. *Autobiography* 134.

19. *Decline and Fall* 9 (1:213).

20. *Decline and Fall* 9 (1:236).

21. *Decline and Fall* 16 (2:81).

22. They have several times been reprinted, most recently (from the Bury edition) as *The Triumph of Christendom in the Roman Empire* (New York: Harper & Row, Torchbooks, 1958).

23. *Decline and Fall* 70 (7:296, n. 101).

24. Gibbon was so moved by it that he published it as part of his *Autobiography* (Saunders ed.), 176–77.

25. John Henry Newman, *An Essay on the Development of Christian Doctrine* (New York: Doubleday, 1960), 35.

26. *Autobiography* 173.

27. *Decline and Fall* 15 (2:2).

28. *Decline and Fall* 13 (1:385).

29. *Decline and Fall* 33 (3:414, n. 48; 457).

30. *Decline and Fall* 11 (1:305, n. 70); italics added.

31. *Decline and Fall* 15 (2:69–70).

32. *Autobiography* 103.

33. *Autobiography* 198.

34. *Decline and Fall* 23 (2:456, n. 70).

35. From those chapters see, for example, *Decline and Fall* 4 (1:92, n. 31); 6 (1:146, n. 71); 12 (1:334–35, n. 58); 14 (1:427, n. 93); 29 (3:238, n. 60).

36. *Decline and Fall* 40 (4:212, 215).

37. *Decline and Fall* 32 (3:382).

38. *Decline and Fall* Bury's Appendix 1 (4:515–17).

39. See, for example, *Decline and Fall* 40 (4:213, nn. 24–26).

40. *Autobiography* 195, adopting the emendation "fate" for "date."

41. Evelyn Waugh, *Helena. A Novel* (Boston: Little, Brown, 1950), 107, 115–16.

4. History as Divine Apocalypse

1. *Decline and Fall* 15 (2:25–26).

2. *Decline and Fall* 25 (3:29, n. 80).

3. Jerome *Commentary on Ezekiel* pr.

4. Jerome *Commentary on Ezekiel* 3.pr.

5. Jerome *Epistles* 126.2.

6. Jerome *Epistles* 127.12.

7. Gordon Williams, *Techniques and Ideas in the "Aeneid"* (New Haven, CT: Yale University Press, 1983), 247.

8. Virgil *Aeneid* 2.363.

9. Jerome *Epistles* 128.5.

10. Jerome *Epistles* 122, 123, 126, 127, 128, 130. See the studies of Jean Rémy Palanque, "Saint Jerome and the Barbarians," and of Edwin A. Quain, "Saint Jerome as a Humanist," in Francis Xavier Murphy, ed., *A Monument to Saint Jerome* (New York: Sheed & Ward, 1952).

11. Virgil *Aeneid* 2.368–69.
12. Jerome *Epistles* 60.18.
13. *Decline and Fall* 30 (3:237).
14. *Decline and Fall* 30 (3:250).
15. *Decline and Fall* 30 (3:277).
16. *Decline and Fall* 29 (3:224–25).
17. Jerome *Epistles* 123.17.
18. Virgil *Aeneid* 6.625–27.
19. *Interpreter's Dictionary of the Bible,* 4 vols. (New York: Abingdon, 1962), 1:140–43.
20. Jerome *Epistles* 123.16.
21. Jerome *Commentary on Jeremiah* 25.26; *Commentary on Daniel* 7.7–8.
22. *Decline and Fall* 15 (2:27).
23. Jaroslav Pelikan, "The Eschatology of Tertullian," *Church History* 21 (1952): 108–22.
24. Tertullian *On Flight in Persecution* 12.
25. Tertullian *Against Marcion* 5.16.
26. Tertullian *On the Resurrection of the Flesh* 24.
27. *Decline and Fall* 15 (2:63).
28. Johannes Quasten, *Patrology,* 3 vols. thus far (Westminster, MD: Newman, 1951–), 2:256.
29. Tertullian *Apology* 32.
30. Tertullian *Apology* 39.
31. Tertullian *To Scapula* 2.
32. *Decline and Fall* 71 (7:317).
33. *Decline and Fall* 25 (3:42).
34. *Decline and Fall* 15 (2:25).
35. Jerome *Epistles* 46.12.
36. *Decline and Fall* 31 (3:325).
37. Jerome *Epistles* 127.
38. Jerome *Epistles* 107.2.
39. J. N. D. Kelly, *Jerome* (London: Duckworth, 1975), 3.
40. See my note, *The Preaching of Augustine* (Philadelphia: Fortress, 1973), 139, n. 23.
41. Peter Brown, *Augustine of Hippo: A Biography* (London: Faber & Faber, 1967), 22.
42. Jerome *Commentary on Isaiah* 19:5–11.
43. Jerome *Epistles* 53.7.
44. Augustine *City of God* 10.27.
45. Augustine *Epistles* 137.12; see also *Epistles* 258.5.
46. See Gibbon's sardonic reference to it, *Decline and Fall* 36 (4:33, n. 86).
47. Jerome *Epistles* 22.30.
48. Quain, "Saint Jerome as a Humanist," 228.
49. Jerome *Epistles* 46.12.
50. Kelly *Jerome* 189.
51. Jerome *Against Jovinian* 2.38.
52. *Decline and Fall* 21 (2:394).

5. The Register of Human Follies, Crimes, and Misfortunes

1. Jerome *Against the Pelagians* 2.26.
2. *Webster's New Dictionary of Synonyms* (Springfield, MA: G. & C. Merriam, 1968), 138, quoting *Decline and Fall* 71 (7:301).
3. *Decline and Fall* 3 (1:76–78).
4. Within chapter 14, for example, he speaks of the "many crimes and misfortunes occasioned by the passions of the Roman princes" (Bury 1:412), but only a few pages later he says concerning the wife and daughter of Diocletian: "We lament their misfortunes, we cannot discover their crimes" (Bury 1:429). Or again, in chapter 31 (Bury 3:321): "The crime and folly of the court of Ravenna was expiated a third time by the calamities of Rome."
5. Therefore, while "misfortune" is sometimes used as we are using it here to refer to calamities brought on by nature, it can refer as well to "deserved misfortunes on the side of the Roman emperor." *Decline and Fall* 10 (1:269).
6. *Decline and Fall* 15 (2:4).
7. *Decline and Fall* 12 (1:347 and n. 109).
8. *Decline and Fall* 11 (1:302); 50 (5:378–79).
9. *Decline and Fall* 9 (1:215–16 and n. 12); for the same contrast between North and South, but in the opposite direction, see 52 (6:8).
10. *Decline and Fall* 69 (7:210).
11. *Decline and Fall* 13 (1:370).
12. *Decline and Fall* 14 (1:404); see also 31 (3:287); 49 (5:265).
13. *Decline and Fall* 14 (1:437 and n. 118); also 32 (3:372, n. 37, and 384).
14. *Decline and Fall* 12 (1:334).
15. *Decline and Fall* 13 (1:358).
16. *Decline and Fall* 13 (1:359–60).
17. *Decline and Fall* 10 (1:265). See also 35 (3:459); 36 (4:12; 36); 46 (5:94); 48 (5:181).
18. *Decline and Fall* 10 (1:281); also 12 (1:340–41).
19. *Decline and Fall* 43 (4:432–40).
20. *Oxford English Dictionary* (Oxford: Oxford University Press, 1933ff.), 1:91, s.v. "Act."
21. *Decline and Fall* 3 (1:74).
22. *Decline and Fall* 6 (1:157).
23. *Decline and Fall* 14 (1:420–21); 11 (1:298); 9 (1:224, n. 43).
24. *Decline and Fall* 28 (3:215, n. 96).
25. *Decline and Fall* 10 (1:279–80); 28 (3:198).
26. *Decline and Fall* 9 (1:229).
27. *Decline and Fall* 7 (1:193).
28. *Decline and Fall* 15 (2:22).
29. *Decline and Fall* 25 (3:54).
30. *Decline and Fall* 32 (3:359); and especially 49 (5:244–310), where the term "superstition" appears on one page after another.
31. *Decline and Fall* 13 (1:392–93).
32. *Decline and Fall* 8 (1:201).
33. *Decline and Fall* 47 (5:97–98).

34. *Decline and Fall* 15 (2:56; 19–32).
35. *Decline and Fall* 6 (1:126); 71 (7:308, n. 25).
36. *Decline and Fall* 14 (1:434); 27 (3:164).
37. *Decline and Fall* 3 (1:77); for a similar description of Justinian, see 47 (5:133).
38. *Decline and Fall* 4 (1:83); 3 (1:76).
39. *Decline and Fall* 9 (1:227).
40. *Decline and Fall* 3 (1:75, n. 48); 4 (1:92).
41. *Decline and Fall* 11 (1:304); 48 (5:186); 10 (1:254); 6 (1:144).
42. *Decline and Fall* 12 (1:325); 6 (1:156).
43. *Decline and Fall* 44 (4:505–6).
44. *Decline and Fall* 3 (1:68).
45. *Decline and Fall* 6 (1:146–47).
46. *Decline and Fall* 12 (1:342).
47. *Decline and Fall* 7 (1:171–72).
48. *Decline and Fall* 40 (4:220).
49. *Decline and Fall* 48 (5:231).
50. *Decline and Fall* 31 (3:320).
51. *Decline and Fall* 6 (1:157), together with Bury's note 96, correcting that judgment of Caracalla's motives.
52. *Decline and Fall* 35 (3:464).
53. *Decline and Fall* 5 (1:116); see also 25 (3:53); 26 (3:118); 36 (4:9).
54. *Decline and Fall* 3 (1:79).
55. *Decline and Fall* 6 (1:135).
56. *Decline and Fall* 14 (1:402).
57. *Decline and Fall* 6 (1:130); 53 (6:78, n. 39).
58. *Decline and Fall* 2 (1:39–42); see also 31 (3:293–94); 33 (3:429).
59. *Decline and Fall* 31 (3:312–13).
60. *Decline and Fall* 12 (1:335).
61. *Decline and Fall* 71 (7:318–20); 30 (3:258–59); 38 (4:132–33).
62. *Decline and Fall* 31 (3:286); 2 (1:39).

6. The Founding of the Christian Empire

1. Bede *A History of the English Church and People* 1.11.
2. *Decline and Fall* 21 (2:343, n. 42); 32 (3:376, n. 44).
3. *Decline and Fall* 23 (2:470, n. 119); 31 (3:319); 32 (3:386, n. 72); 21 (2:384, n. 154).
4. *Decline and Fall* 28 (3:197); 33 (3:411).
5. *Decline and Fall* 47 (5:138).
6. Under the general title "Divine Providence and the Roman Empire: A Positive Eastern Christian Interpretation of Recent History," Walter Kaegi presents some very helpful insights into their histories in his fine monograph *Byzantium and the Decline of Rome* (Princeton, NJ: Princeton University Press, 1968).
7. Socrates Scholasticus *Ecclesiastical History* 7.10.
8. *Decline and Fall* 31 (3:318).
9. Sozomen *Ecclesiastical History* 9.6–10.
10. *Decline and Fall* 31 (3:322).

11. Sozomen *Ecclesiastical History* 9.9.
12. *Decline and Fall* 31 (3:323).
13. Kaegi, *Byzantium and the Decline of Rome,* 178.
14. Sozomen *Ecclesiastical History* 9.6.
15. Sozomen *Ecclesiastical History* 9.5.
16. Sozomen *Ecclesiastical History* 9.6.
17. Sozomen *Ecclesiastical History* 9.3.
18. Sozomen *Ecclesiastical History* ded.
19. Sozomen *Ecclesiastical History* ded.
20. Socrates Scholasticus *Ecclesiastical History* 7.42.
21. Gregory of Nyssa *The Beatitudes* 2.
22. Theodoret *Ecclesiastical History* 5.34.
23. *Decline and Fall* 20 (2:327); 32 (3:375); all of this despite his being *"almost a stranger to the voluminous sermons of Chrysostom,"* 32 (3:375, n. 42).
24. John Chrysostom *Homilies on Matthew* 15.
25. Jaroslav Pelikan, *The Preaching of Chrysostom* (Philadelphia: Fortress Press, 1967), 17.
26. Theodoret *Ecclesiastical History* 1, pr.
27. Edward Schwartz, "Über Kirchengeschichte," *Gesammelte Schriften,* 1, 2d ed. (Berlin: Walter de Gruyter, 1963), 125.
28. Socrates *Ecclesiastical History* 1.16.
29. *Decline and Fall* 20 (2:321, n. 104).
30. Eusebius *Life of Constantine* 1.12.
31. Eusebius *Ecclesiastical History* 10.4.6.
32. Eusebius *Ecclesiastical History* 9.9.8, quoting the Septuagint version of Exod. 15:10.
33. Judah Goldin, *The Song at the Sea* (New Haven, CT: Yale University Press, 1971), 31.
34. Eusebius *Ecclesiastical History* 9.9.5, quoting Exod. 15:5.
35. *Decline and Fall* 14 (1:441).
36. Quoted in Eusebius *Ecclesiastical History* 9.9.11 (translation by Ramsay MacMullen).
37. Eusebius *Ecclesiastical History* 10.9.6.
38. Eusebius *Ecclesiastical History* 1.1.1.
39. Eusebius *Ecclesiastical History* 7.32.32.
40. Jaroslav Pelikan, *The Finality of Jesus Christ in an Age of Universal History* (London: Lutterworth Press, 1965), 48–57.
41. Jacob Burckhardt, *Die Zeit Constantins des Grossen* (Vienna: Phaidon, n.d.), 242, 249.
42. J. B. Lightfoot, *The Apostolic Fathers,* 3 vols. in 6 (London: Macmillan, 1890), 1:165.
43. Eusebius, *"The Ecclesiastical History" and "The Martyrs of Palestine",* ed. Hugh Jackson Lawlor and John Ernest Leonard Oulton (London: S.P.C.K., 1954), 2:13, 40–46.
44. Socrates *Ecclesiastical History* 1.16.
45. Council of Chalcedon, canon 28.
46. Thomas Owen Martin, "The Twenty-Eighth Canon of Chalcedon: A Background Note," in Aloys Grillmeier and Heinrich Bacht, eds., *Das Konzil von Chalkedon,* 3 vols. (Würzburg: Echter Verlag, 1951), 2:433–58.

47. Shirley Jackson Case, *The Social Triumph of the Ancient Church* (New York: Harper & Brothers, 1933), 196.
48. Sozomen *Ecclesiastical History* 2.3.
49. *Decline and Fall* 17 (2:147).
50. Steven Runciman, *A History of the Crusades,* 3 vols. (Cambridge: Cambridge University Press, 1951–1954), 3:130.
51. *Decline and Fall* 17 (2:146–47).
52. Karl Holl, "Die kirchliche Bedeutung Konstantinopels im Mittelalter," *Gesammelte Aufsätze zur Kirchengeschichte,* vol. 2, *Der Osten* (Tübingen: J. C. B. Mohr (Paul Siebeck), 1928), 409–17.

7. The Inevitable Effect of Immoderate Greatness

1. *Decline and Fall* 38 (4:161).
2. For others, see the discussion in chapter 3.
3. *Decline and Fall* 41 (4:293).
4. *Decline and Fall* 3 (1:78).
5. *Decline and Fall* 44 (4:442).
6. *Decline and Fall* 39 (4:188).
7. *Decline and Fall* 5 (1:124, 118).
8. *Decline and Fall* 3 (1:78).
9. *Decline and Fall* 29 (3:233); 12 (1:318–19).
10. *Decline and Fall* 40 (4:268).
11. *Decline and Fall* 37 (4:13); 30 (3:240); 43 (4:417).
12. *Decline and Fall* 24 (2:501).
13. *Decline and Fall* 31 (3:295); see also 26 (3:124–25) on the combination (reminiscent of Plato's *Laws* 709) of "prudence," "fortune," and the ability "to seize, and to improve, every favourable circumstance."
14. *Decline and Fall* 5 (1:115); in his footnote Gibbon describes Julius as "at the same time, making love to Cleopatra, sustaining a siege against the power of Egypt, and conversing with the sages of the country."
15. *Decline and Fall* 5 (1:111); 6 (1:139–40).
16. *Decline and Fall* 13 (1:351).
17. *Decline and Fall* 12 (1:328, 330).
18. *Decline and Fall* 10 (1:268); 8 (1:211).
19. *Decline and Fall* 17 (2:179); 19 (2:279); 25 (3:48).
20. *Decline and Fall* 7 (1:194).
21. *Decline and Fall* 6 (1:165–66).
22. *Decline and Fall* 31 (3:288–89).
23. *Decline and Fall* 13 (1:380–81); 29 (3:216); 20 (2:301).
24. *Decline and Fall* 13 (1:356).
25. *Decline and Fall* 10 (1:276).
26. *Decline and Fall* 17 (2:176–77).
27. *Decline and Fall* 5 (1:103).
28. *Decline and Fall* 1 (1:15, n. 61).
29. *Decline and Fall* 6 (1:136, 141, 153).
30. *Decline and Fall* 8 (1:195).
31. *Decline and Fall* 9 (1:226, 232).

32. *Decline and Fall* 14 (1:416).
33. *Decline and Fall* 10 (1:250); 12 (1:319, 324).
34. *Decline and Fall* 26 (3:130).
35. *Decline and Fall* 5 (1:103–5).
36. *Decline and Fall* 5 (1:106–14).
37. *Decline and Fall* 5 (1:123).
38. *Decline and Fall* 6 (1:153–54); 7 (1:187–89); 14 (1:403, 409, 416).
39. *Decline and Fall* 13 (1:379–80); 14 (1:422–24).
40. *Decline and Fall* 25 (3:59).
41. *Decline and Fall* 31 (3:334).
42. *Decline and Fall* 41 (4:281); also 37 (4:27).
43. *Decline and Fall* 42 (4:352).
44. *Decline and Fall* 24 (2:490).
45. *Decline and Fall* 15 (2:54); 23 (2:476).
46. *Decline and Fall* 33 (3:404).
47. *Decline and Fall* 30 (3:266).
48. *Decline and Fall* 27 (3:187).
49. *Decline and Fall* 49 (5:302).
50. *Decline and Fall* 44 (4:485).
51. *Decline and Fall* 6 (1:160).
52. *Decline and Fall* 6 (1:158, 162).
53. *Decline and Fall* 25 (3:44).
54. *Decline and Fall* 29 (3:221).
55. *Decline and Fall* 14 (1:441).
56. *Decline and Fall* 7 (1:194); 30 (3:263–64); 30 (3:273); 36 (4:39); 50 (5:311); 52 (6:1).
57. *Decline and Fall* 24 (2:483–84).
58. *Decline and Fall* 36 (4:56); 31 (3:302).
59. *Decline and Fall* 12 (1:336).
60. *Decline and Fall* 36 (4:55).
61. *Decline and Fall* 36 (4:1).
62. *Decline and Fall* 14 (1:402).
63. *Decline and Fall* 6 (1:162); 6 (1:164–65); 13 (1:384).
64. *Decline and Fall* 17 (2:160–74, 182–90).
65. *Decline and Fall* 6 (1:157).
66. *Decline and Fall* 17 (2:185).
67. *Decline and Fall* 25 (3:46).
68. *Decline and Fall* 36 (4:19).
69. *Decline and Fall* 26 (3:132, n. 143); italics his.
70. William Shakespeare, *Julius Caesar,* act 1, sc. 2, lines 139–41.
71. *Decline and Fall* 34 (3:419).
72. *Decline and Fall* 10 (1:277–78).
73. *Decline and Fall* 7 (1:194).
74. *Decline and Fall* 1 (1:2–3).
75. *Decline and Fall* 12 (1:336).
76. *Decline and Fall* 43 (4:388).
77. Gilbert Murray, *Five Stages of Greek Religion* (Garden City, NY: Doubleday, Anchor Books, [1925]), xiii.

8. The Terrestrial Glory of an Excellent Empire

1. *Decline and Fall* 33 (3:407).
2. *Decline and Fall* 31 (3:323); on Augustine's "insults" to his adversaries, see also 24 (2:508).
3. *Decline and Fall* 71 (7:307, n. 22); 30 (3:266, n. 79).
4. *Decline and Fall* 31 (3:338–39); 10 (1:256).
5. *Decline and Fall* 31 (3:333), quoting from Orosius, *History Against the Pagans* 7.43.
6. Peter Brown, *Augustine of Hippo: A Biography* (London: Faber & Faber, 1967), 296.
7. *Decline and Fall* 33 (3:411).
8. *Decline and Fall* 35 (3:451, n. 12).
9. *Decline and Fall*, Bury's "Appendix 1. Authorities" (3:481–91).
10. Augustine *City of God* 5.15.
11. Jaroslav Pelikan, *The Christian Tradition: A History of the Development of Doctrine*, 5 vols. (Chicago: University of Chicago Press, 1971–), 1:318–31.
12. Augustine *City of God* 1.pr.
13. Augustine *City of God* 18.1.
14. Gibbon cites "two columns, with a Phoenician inscription," reported by Sallust, identifying the Moors as descendants of the Canaanites "who fled from the robber Joshua." He comments: "I believe in the columns—I doubt the inscription—and I reject the pedigree" *Decline and Fall* 41 (4:296, n. 48).
15. Augustine *City of God* 18.2, quoting Sallust *The War Against Catiline* 8.
16. On Augustine's use of Varro and the way the *City of God* functions as a response to him, see Jaroslav Pelikan, *The Mystery of Continuity: Time and History, Memory and Eternity, in the Thought of Saint Augustine* (Charlottesville, VA: University of Virginia Press, 1986), 40–44.
17. Augustine *City of God* 18.8.
18. Augustine *City of God* 18.10; 18.27.
19. Augustine *City of God* 18.31.
20. *Decline and Fall* 15 (2:66).
21. *Decline and Fall* 33 (3:432, n. 38).
22. Sisela Bok, *Lying: Moral Choice in Public and Private Life* (New York: Vintage Books, 1978), 32–46.
23. Augustine *City of God* 20.23.
24. Lactantius *On the Deaths of the Persecutors* 15–17.
25. *Decline and Fall* 20 (2:307, n. 57).
26. Lactantius *Divine Institutes* 7.16.
27. Lactantius *Divine Institutes* 7.15.
28. Augustine *City of God* 20.19.
29. Augustine *Against the Letters of Petilian the Donatist* 3.2.3.
30. Augustine *City of God* 20.19.
31. Augustine *City of God* 20.7.
32. Augustine *City of God* 20.9.
33. Hermann Reuter, *Augustinische Studien* (Gotha: F. A. Perthes, 1887), 114.
34. Augustine *City of God* 5.25.

35. Augustine *City of God* 5.21.
36. Brown *Augustine of Hippo* 291.
37. *Decline and Fall* 20 (2:314, n. 83).
38. Augustine *City of God* 5.26.
39. Augustine *City of God* 5.12.
40. Augustine *City of God* 5.15.
41. Augustine *City of God* 2.29.
42. Augustine *City of God* 4.4.
43. Heinrich Scholz, *Glaube und Unglaube in der Weltgeschichte* (Leipzig: J. C. Hinrich'sche Buchhandlung, 1911), 148–54.
44. Augustine *City of God* 1.35; 18.1.
45. Scholz *Glaube und Unglaube* 109.
46. Augustine *City of God* 20.9.
47. Augustine *City of God* 1.35.
48. See Pelikan *The Mystery of Continuity* 90–105.
49. Bernard McGinn, "Angel Pope and Papal Antichrist," *Church History* 47 (1978):155–73.
50. Henri Xavier Arquillière, *L'augustinisme politique: Essai sur la formation des théories politiques du moyen-âge,* 2d ed. (Paris: J. Vrin, 1955).
51. Einhard *The Life of Charlemagne* 3.24.
52. *Decline and Fall* 1 (1:27).

9. The Inestimable Gifts of Roman Civilization

1. *Decline and Fall* 31 (3:323).
2. Augustine *City of God* 5.15.
3. *Decline and Fall* 40 (4:265).
4. *Decline and Fall* 38 (4:167–69). For Gibbon's use of "inestimable gifts," see also 36 (4:2).
5. *Decline and Fall* 1 (1:1).
6. *Decline and Fall,* Bury's "Introduction" (1:xxxv).
7. *Decline and Fall* 34 (3:426).
8. *Decline and Fall* 44 (4:446, 457).
9. *Decline and Fall* 5 (1:125).
10. *Decline and Fall* 12 (1:321).
11. *Decline and Fall* 32 (3:366).
12. *Decline and Fall* 44 (4:461, 441).
13. *Decline and Fall,* Bury's "Introduction" (1:lii).
14. *Decline and Fall* 44 (4:463).
15. *Decline and Fall* 2 (1:28).
16. *Decline and Fall* 16 (2:71).
17. *Decline and Fall* 37 (4:95), quoting Bede *A History of the English Church and People* 1.26.
18. *Decline and Fall* 21 (2:391–92).
19. See the thoughtful analysis of Hermann Doerries, *Constantine and Religious Liberty,* trans. Roland H. Bainton (New Haven, CT: Yale University Press, 1960).
20. *Decline and Fall* 27 (3:151–55).

21. *Decline and Fall* 28 (3:188–89).
22. *Decline and Fall* 20 (2:320–24).
23. *Decline and Fall* 20 (2:323–24).
24. *Decline and Fall* 14 (1:434).
25. *Decline and Fall* 44 (4:472–76).
26. *Decline and Fall* 14 (1:432–34).
27. *Decline and Fall* 17 (2:172–74).
28. *Decline and Fall* 38 (4:122–26).
29. *Decline and Fall* 38 (4:140) on the Franks; 38 (4:143) on Spain; 38 (4:152) on Britain; 44 (5:29–30) on the Lombards.
30. Bury's note to *Decline and Fall* 38 (4:122, n. 71).
31. *Decline and Fall* 47 (5:144).
32. *Decline and Fall* 39 (4:182); 34 (3:428).
33. *Decline and Fall* 53 (6:102–3); also 21 (2:253) and 47 (5:144) on the relative merits of Latin and Greek.
34. *Decline and Fall* 37 (4:79–80).
35. *Decline and Fall* 26 (3:130).
36. *Decline and Fall* 38 (4:99, 140).
37. *Decline and Fall* 45 (5:24–25).
38. *Decline and Fall* 11 (1:295, n. 28).
39. *Decline and Fall* 44 (4:467).
40. *Decline and Fall* 45 (5, 32, 34).
41. *Decline and Fall* 1 (1:21); italics original.
42. *Decline and Fall* 37 (4:57–75).
43. *Decline and Fall* 37 (4:69).
44. See in particular *Decline and Fall* 15 (2:19); 1 (1:30).
45. *Decline and Fall* 40 (4:262).
46. *Decline and Fall* 20 (2:326–27).
47. *Decline and Fall* 27 (3:158).
48. *Decline and Fall* 33 (3:407).
49. *Decline and Fall* 27 (3:155).
50. *Decline and Fall* 32 (3:369–70).
51. *Decline and Fall* 39 (4:197–203).
52. *Decline and Fall* 12 (1:341).
53. *Decline and Fall* 37 (4:63).
54. *Decline and Fall* 27 (3:155–56).
55. *Decline and Fall* 45 (5:34–35).
56. *Decline and Fall* 25 (3:2–3); italics his, quoting the emperor Jovian.
57. *Decline and Fall* 21 (2:352).
58. *Decline and Fall* 23 (2:473).
59. *Decline and Fall* 21 (2:348, 340, 380).
60. *Decline and Fall* 21 (2:371).
61. *Decline and Fall* 21 (2:362).
62. *Decline and Fall* 38 (4:169, 139–40, 163).
63. *Decline and Fall* 37 (4:80).

Index of Names

(The names of Constantine and Gibbon are mentioned, or at least implied, on almost every page, and are therefore not listed here. Figures from antiquity are identified by dates of death, Roman emperors and popes by years of reign.)